# 2 SAMUEL

*David's Heart Revealed*

John MacArthur

THOMAS NELSON
*Since 1798*

MacArthur Bible Studies

2 Samuel: David's Heart Revealed

Published in Nashville, Tennessee, by Nelson Books, an imprint of Thomas Nelson. Nelson Books and Thomas Nelson are registered trademarks of HarperCollins Christian Publishing, Inc.

Originally published in association with the literary agency of Wolgemuth & Associates, Inc. Original layout, design, and writing assistance by Gregory C. Benoit Publishing, Old Mystic, Connecticut.

"Unleashing God's Truth, One Verse at a Time®" is a trademark of Grace to You. All rights reserved.

Thomas Nelson titles may be purchased in bulk for educational, business, fundraising, or sales promotional use. For information, please e-mail SpecialMarkets@ThomasNelson.com.

ISBN 978-07180-3474-0

First Printing January 2016 / Printed in the United States of America

HB 01.03.2024

# CONTENTS

*Introduction*                                        v

1. Uniting a Divided House                            1
   *2 Samuel 2:1–3:30*

2. Obedience and Blessing                            13
   *2 Samuel 6:1–23*

3. A Throne Established Forever                      25
   *2 Samuel 7:1–29*

4. Remembering Past Promises                         37
   *2 Samuel 9:1–13*

5. David's Acts of Sin                               49
   *2 Samuel 11:1–27*

6. David's Sins Are Revealed                         61
   *2 Samuel 12:1–25*

7. Trouble in David's House                          73
   *2 Samuel 13:1–39*

8. Absalom's Rebellion                               85
   *2 Samuel 15:1–37*

9. Absalom's Defeat 97

*2 Samuel 18:1–19:15*

10. A Second Rebellion 109

*2 Samuel 19:16–20:26*

11. The Man After God's Heart 121

*2 Samuel 22:1–23:7*

12. Reviewing Key Principles 133

# INTRODUCTION

The Israelites had cried out for a king so they could be like the pagan nations around them, and God had answered by raising up a man named Saul. Unfortunately, Saul was not faithful to the Lord, and thus was not faithful to the Lord's people. When he refused to repent, God rejected him and chose a new ruler for Israel. This man was David, and while he would be Israel's second king, he would be the first king to follow after God's own heart. The Lord Himself said of him, "I have found . . . a man after My own heart, who will do all My will" (Acts 13:22).

Yet David was also a great sinner. It wasn't long after he ascended to the throne that he committed both adultery and murder—and then tried to cover it up. This raises the obvious question: *How can an adulterous murderer be called a man after God's own heart?* This is the great question of David's life and, of course, every Christian's life as well. How can an ungodly person—as each of us are—be seen by God as faithful?

In these twelve studies, we will answer this question by examining the biblical events depicted in the book of 2 Samuel. We will meet a variety of memorable characters, including Joab, the leader of Israel's army who was both a shrewd military general and a treacherous assassin; Mephibosheth, Saul's grandson, who was lame in both feet; Absalom, who staged a rebellion and attempted to usurp the throne of Israel; and, of course, we will get to know more about the life of King David. We will witness the terrible pain within David's household when three of his sons die tragically, and we will also examine the nature of sin, the importance of repentance, and the value of obedience.

Through it all, we will learn some precious truths about the character of God, and we will see His great faithfulness in keeping His promises. Ultimately, as we witness these events in the life of King David, we will learn from his example what it truly means to be a person after God's own heart.

## Title

First and Second Samuel were considered one book in the earliest Hebrew manuscripts. They were later divided into two books by the translators of the Greek version, known as the Septuagint. This division was later followed by the Latin Vulgate, English translations, and modern Hebrew Bibles. The earliest Hebrew manuscripts titled the one book *Samuel*, after the man God used to establish the kingship in Israel.

## Author and Date

Jewish tradition ascribed the writing of Samuel to the prophet himself or to Samuel, Nathan, and Gad (based on 1 Chronicles 29:29). However, Samuel cannot be the writer, because his death is recorded in 1 Samuel 25:1, before the events associated with David's reign take place. Further, Nathan and Gad were prophets of the Lord during David's lifetime and would not have been alive when the book was written. Thus, though the written records of these three prophets could have been used for information in the writing of 1 and 2 Samuel, the human author of these books is unknown. The work comes to the reader as an anonymous writing.

The books of Samuel contain no clear indication of the date of composition. However, it is clear the author wrote them after the division of the kingdom between Israel and Judah in 931 BC due to the many references to Israel and Judah as distinct entities. Also, the statement concerning Ziklag's belonging "to the kings of Judah to this day" in 1 Samuel 27:6 gives clear evidence of a post-Solomonic date of writing. There is no such clarity concerning how late the date of writing could be, but most likely it was penned before the exile during the period of the divided kingdom (c. 931–722 BC).

## BACKGROUND AND SETTING

The majority of the action in 1 and 2 Samuel takes place in and around the central highlands of Israel. The nation was largely concentrated in an area that ran about ninety miles from the hill country of Ephraim in the north to the hill country of Judah in the south, and between fifteen to thirty-five miles east to west. The major cities of 1 and 2 Samuel were found in these central highlands: Shiloh, the residence of Eli and the tabernacle; Ramah, the hometown of Samuel; Gibeah, the headquarters of Saul; Bethlehem, the birthplace of David; Hebron, David's capital when he ruled over Judah; and Jerusalem, the ultimate "city of David."

The events in 1 and 2 Samuel occurred between the years c. 1105 BC (the birth of Samuel in 1 Samuel 1:1–28) and c. 971 BC (the last words of David in 2 Samuel 23:1–7). Thus, the books span about 135 years of history. During those years, Israel was transformed from a loosely knit group of tribes under judges to a united nation under the reign of a centralized monarchy. The books primarily examine the lives of Samuel (c. 1105–1030 BC); Saul, who reigned c. 1051–1011 BC; and David, who was king of the united monarchy (c. 1011–971 BC).

## HISTORICAL AND THEOLOGICAL THEMES

As 1 Samuel begins, Israel was at a low point spiritually. The priesthood was corrupt, the ark of the covenant was not at the tabernacle, idolatry was being practiced, and the judges were dishonest. Through the influence of Samuel and David, these conditions were reversed. By the end of 2 Samuel, the anger of the Lord had been withdrawn from Israel (see 2 Samuel 24:25).

During the years narrated in 1 and 2 Samuel, the great empires of the ancient world were in a state of weakness. Neither Egypt nor the Mesopotamian powers, Babylon and Assyria, were threats to Israel at this time. The two nations most hostile to the Israelites were the Ammonites to the east and the Philistines to the west. The Ammonites were descendants of Lot (see Genesis 19:38) who lived on the Transjordan plateau. The major contingent of the Philistines had migrated from the Aegean islands and Asia Minor in the twelfth century BC. After being denied access to Egypt, they settled among other Philistines along the Mediterranean coast of Palestine. They controlled the use of iron, which gave them a decided military and economic advantage over Israel.

There are four predominant theological themes in 1 and 2 Samuel. The first is the Davidic covenant. The books are literally framed by two references to the "anointed" king in the prayer of Hannah (see 1 Samuel 2:10) and the song of David (see 2 Samuel 22:51). This is a reference to the Messiah, the King who would triumph over the nations who are opposed to God. According to the Lord's promise, this Messiah would come through the line of David and establish David's throne forever (see 2 Samuel 7:12–16). The events of David's life recorded in Samuel foreshadow the actions of David's greater Son (Christ) in the future.

A second theme is the sovereignty of God. In regard to David, it is particularly evident that nothing can frustrate God's plan to have him rule over Israel. Furthermore, there was nothing David could do to hide his sin with Bathsheba, for the Lord sees all and is in sovereign control over everything that takes place in this world.

A third theme is the work of the Holy Spirit in empowering people for divinely appointed tasks. The Spirit of the Lord came on both Saul and David after their anointing as king (see 1 Samuel 10:10; 16:13). The power of the Holy Spirit brought forth prophecy (see 10:6) and victory in battle (see 11:6). At the end of his life, David was able to say, "The Spirit of the LORD spoke by me, and His word was on my tongue" (2 Samuel 23:2).

A fourth theme centers on the personal and national effects of sin. Saul's disobedience resulted in the Lord's judgment, and he was rejected as king over Israel (see 1 Samuel 13 and 15). In addition, though David was forgiven for his sin of adultery and murder after his confession (see 2 Samuel 12:13), he still suffered the inevitable and devastating consequences of his sin (see 12:14).

## Interpretive Challenges

The books of 1 and 2 Samuel contain a number of interpretive issues that have been widely discussed. The first issue is *which of the ancient manuscripts is closest to the original autograph.* The standard Hebrew (Masoretic) text has been relatively poorly preserved, and the Septuagint often differs from it. Thus, the exact reading of the original autograph in places is hard to determine (see, for example, 1 Samuel 13:1). For this study, the Masoretic text will be assumed to represent the original text unless there is a grammatical or contextual impossibility, which will account for many of the numerical discrepancies.

A second issue is *how to explain the bizarre behavior of the prophets*. It is commonly held that 1 and 2 Samuel present the prophets as ecstatic speakers with bizarre behavior, just like the pagan prophets of the other nations. However, there is nothing in the text that is inconsistent with seeing the prophets as communicators of divine revelation, at times prophesying with musical accompaniment.

A third issue is *how the Holy Spirit ministered before Pentecost*. Passages about the Spirit's ministry, such as 1 Samuel 10:6, 10; 11:6; 16:13–14; 19:20, 23; and 2 Samuel 23:2, do not describe salvation in the New Testament sense but as an empowering by the Lord for His service (see also Judges 3:10; 6:34; 11:29; 13:25; 14:6, 19; 15:14).

A final issue concerns *the identity of David's seed in 2 Samuel 7:12–15 who will establish his kingdom*. It is usually taken as Solomon. However, the New Testament authors refer the words to Jesus, God's Son (see, for example, Hebrews 1:5).

# ISRAEL IN THE TIME OF DAVID

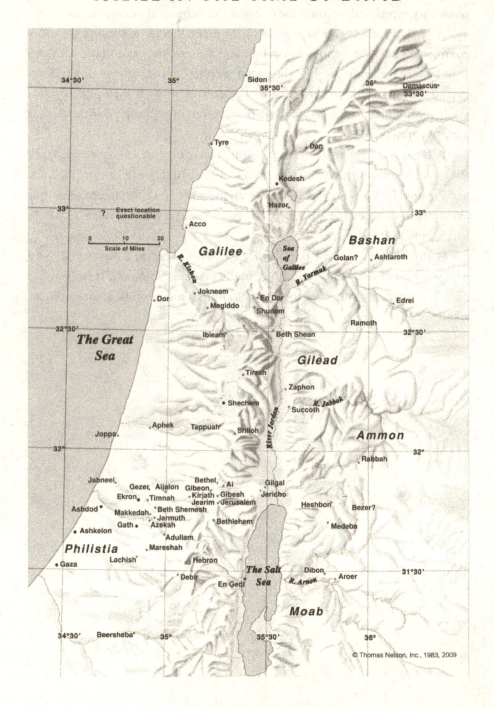

34°30'   35°
Sidon
35°30'   36°   Damascus°
33°30'

Tyre
Dan

Kedesh

33°   ? Exact location questionable   Hazor   33°

Acco

0   10   20
Scale of Miles

Galilee   Sea of Galilee   Bashan
Golan?   Ashtaroth
R. Kishon   R. Yarmuk

Dor   Jokneam
Megiddo   En Dor   Edrei
Shunem
Ramoth

32°30'   Ibleam   Beth Shean   32°30'

The Great Sea   Gilead
Tirzah
Zaphon

Shechem   R. Jabbok
Succoth
Aphek   Tappuah   Shiloh

Joppa   Ammon

32°   River Jordan   32°

Rabbah

Jabneel   Bethel   Ai   Gilgal
Gezer   Aijalon   Gibeon   Jericho
Ekron   Timnah   Kirjath   Gibeah
Jearim   Jerusalem   Heshbon   Bezer?
Ashdod   Makkedah   Beth Shemesh
Jarmuth   Bethlehem   Medeba
Gath   Azekah
Ashkelon   Adullam
Philistia   Mareshah
Lachish   Hebron
Gaza   Dibon   Aroer   31°30'
Debir   The Salt Sea   R. Arnon
En Gedi

Moab

34°30'   Beersheba°   35°   35°30'   36°

© Thomas Nelson, Inc., 1983, 2009

# 1

# Uniting a Divided House
## *2 Samuel 2:1–3:30*

## Drawing Near

What kind of divisions do we find in our government today? What problems emerge when people are divided about who should govern them?

_____

_____

_____

## The Context

During the time of the judges in Israel, the Lord had raised up certain individuals to lead His people against their enemies, settle disputes, and protect the nation. However, when the people looked around and saw that the other nations in Canaan were led by kings, they decided they would be better off if they had a king as well. Instead of relying on God to protect them and raise up their leaders, the Israelites chose to imitate the world around them.

Samuel, Israel's last judge and one of God's great prophets, warned the people that exchanging the Lord for a human monarchy would lead to bad consequences. A king would burden the people with taxes and exploit them for his own gain. Yet the people refused to listen, so the Lord instructed Samuel to anoint a young man named Saul as Israel's first king.

Sadly, Samuel's words of warning were fulfilled. Saul was disobedient to God, and the Lord eventually rejected him as king. In his place God chose another man who—unlike Saul—had his heart turned toward obedience. His name was David, and at the time Samuel anointed him as Israel's next king, he was tending flocks for his father, Jesse, in the land near the town of Bethlehem.

Saul, however, continued to reign for many years. But he didn't reign *well*. He understood that God had rejected him as king, and when he suspected that David was the man whom God had selected to replace him, he spent the remainder of his days trying to eliminate David as a threat. Tragically, Saul died in battle against the Philistines, and all his sons died with him—all except one, a man named Ishbosheth.

This study opens shortly after Saul's death, when David was preparing to take over the kingship. God had just called him to go to Hebron, where he would be anointed king over Judah. But Saul's sole survivor, Ishbosheth, felt the throne was his by birthright, and the nation was divided in its loyalties.

## KEYS TO THE TEXT

Read 2 Samuel 2:1–3:30, noting the key words and phrases indicated below.

> DAVID'S SECOND ANOINTING: *After the death of King Saul, the Lord directs David to go to the city of Hebron, where he will be anointed king over the tribe of Judah.*

2:1. DAVID INQUIRED OF THE LORD: After the death of Saul, David was no longer a wanted man and could move about the land freely as the Lord directed him. A contrast can be seen here between Saul, who inquired of the Lord but the Lord would not answer (see 1 Samuel 28:6), and David, who inquired of the Lord and the Lord gave him direction.

CITIES OF JUDAH: David sought guidance from God about where to start his reign. He first asked if he should begin in the southern area of Judah. The Lord responded affirmatively, so David sought a more precise destination. The nucleus of David's future government would come from the cities of Judah.

To Hebron: God strategically chose Hebron, which had the highest elevation of any town in Judah, to be the initial location of David's rule over Israel. Hebron was located twenty miles south-southwest of Jerusalem and was the place where Abraham had lived long before (see Genesis 13:18). Caleb had received Hebron when Israel occupied the land of Canaan after their wilderness wanderings (see Judges 1:20).

2. Ahinoam the Jezreelitess, and Abigail the widow: David had married these two women during the time he was on the run from Saul. Ahinoam bore David his first son, named Amnon. The Amalekites had captured both her and Abigail, the former wife of Nabal, when David was off at war, but David had later recovered them (see 1 Samuel 30).

4. anointed David king: David had already been privately anointed king by Samuel, but this anointing recognized his rule in the southern area of Judah. Later, he would be anointed as king over all Israel (see 2 Samuel 5:3).

men of Jabesh Gilead: The people of Jabesh, a city of Israel located east of the Jordan River, had demonstrated their loyalty to Saul by giving him a proper burial.

7. your master Saul is dead: David referred to Saul as "your master" so as not to antagonize the men of Jabesh Gilead. He sought to win Israel over to his side, not force them into submission.

> COMPETITION FOR THE THRONE: *Saul's only remaining son raises himself up as heir to Saul's throne, effectively dividing the nation of Israel into two factions.*

8. Abner the son of Ner: Abner was King Saul's cousin and the leader of the Israelite army. He remained loyal to Saul's house even though God had already anointed David to be the next king. His loyalty was misplaced at this point, but he eventually agreed to serve David as faithfully as he had served Saul.

Ishbosheth: This was Saul's only surviving son—the others had all been killed in Saul's last battle against the Philistines. His name means "man of shame." Abner put him on the throne as king over the northern tribes of Israel and the eastern tribes across the Jordan.

Mahanaim: Ishbosheth established himself in this town east of the Jordan River and reigned there for two years. This was the same city where Jacob had seen the angels while on his way to Penuel (see Genesis 32:2). It was appointed a Levitical city from the territory of Gad and later became a haven for David while he was fleeing from Absalom.

9. KING OVER GILEAD: The areas listed in this verse under Ishbosheth's reign include most of Israel.

10. ONLY THE HOUSE OF JUDAH FOLLOWED DAVID: A natural opposition arose between the tribe of Judah and the rest of Israel, as Judah was under the reign of David while the rest of Israel recognized the reign of Ishbosheth. David's family was from Judah, and the tribe would remain loyal to him throughout his kingship and beyond.

11. SEVEN YEARS AND SIX MONTHS: Several years passed before Ishbosheth assumed the throne of Israel, so that Ishbosheth's two-year reign came at the end of David's seven-year-and-six-month reign over Judah. It must have taken Ishbosheth about five years to regain the northern territory from the Philistines.

12. GIBEON: During the time of Joshua, Gibeon was an important city. Its people had probably sided with David because Saul had broken a treaty with the Gibeonites and acted treacherously toward them.

13. JOAB THE SON OF ZERUIAH: Joab was David's nephew and the leader of his army. Although Ishbosheth and David sat on the thrones of their respective territories, Joab and Abner truly wielded the power and control by leading the military forces.

*THE TRAGEDY OF CIVIL WAR: Two great generals, Abner and Joab, attempt to prevent all-out warfare, but it proves unavoidable.*

14. LET THE YOUNG MEN NOW ARISE: Abner proposed a combat of champions, twelve from each side, rather than a full-scale war. This was a sensible suggestion so far as it went, as the outcome of the combat, had it been decisive, would have prevented civil war. The problem was that Abner and the men of Israel should have submitted to the kingship of David, since he was the man God had anointed to sit on the throne over all Israel. Abner's plan failed, and the civil war erupted despite his suggestion.

18. THE THREE SONS OF ZERUIAH: Zeruiah was David's sister and the mother of Joab, Abishai, and Asahel. Abishai was an aide to David throughout his rise to power. He had been with David when he had the opportunity to kill

King Saul and had encouraged his murder, but David would not allow it (see 1 Samuel 26:8). Asahel was another of Joab's brothers, and the tragic story that follows reveals that he was a man of character and determination.

19. ASAHEL PURSUED ABNER: Asahel was pursuing Abner in battle, and had he killed this general of the opposing side, it would have immediately ended the conflict. He was clearly out of his league fighting Abner, as will be seen, yet he refused to turn aside from the pursuit. In many ways he was reminiscent of David, who did not hesitate to face the giant Goliath in a single combat that brought great victory to God's people.

21. TAKE HIS ARMOR: For Asahel, obtaining the armor of the enemy general, Abner, would have represented a great trophy. He was ambitious to get it, but Abner suggested he take the armor of some other soldier for his trophy.

22. TURN ASIDE FROM FOLLOWING ME: Abner showed himself to be a man of character in this sad episode. He did not want to kill a young man of Asahel's quality, so he tried repeatedly to dissuade him from battle. But the seeds of division were already sown. Division is the work of the devil, and when God's people are divided against one another, only tragedy can result. Rather than fighting the enemy of their souls, godly men and women attack one another. In doing so, they waste their efforts, just as Abner and Asahel did fighting against each other.

23. DIED ON THE SPOT: This terrible tragedy would have equally terrible long-term consequences. Joab never forgave Abner for killing his brother, even though it had been done in battle.

25. THE CHILDREN OF BENJAMIN: One of the twelve tribes of Israel. It was also Saul's tribe, and they had remained steadfastly loyal to him throughout his turbulent reign.

26. SHALL THE SWORD DEVOUR FOREVER: As Abner had earlier proposed that the hostilities begin, he now proposed that they cease.

*ABNER'S CHANGE OF ALLEGIANCE: As time passes, Abner begins to make his own move to secure the throne of Israel. This creates a rift between him and Ishbosheth.*

3:1. THERE WAS A LONG WAR BETWEEN THE HOUSE OF SAUL AND THE HOUSE OF DAVID: Many tribes of Israel continued to support the house of Saul rather than submitting to David as their king. The Lord had publicly anointed him and told the people, through Samuel, that he was God's selected ruler, yet David still had to establish his throne by force.

7. SAUL HAD A CONCUBINE, WHOSE NAME WAS RIZPAH: By taking Rizpah, Abner was making a clear statement to the people that he would take the place of Saul. Taking the king's concubine was a statement of power and rightful claim to the throne.

8. ABNER BECAME VERY ANGRY: Abner resented Ishbosheth's reaction and, compelled by revenge, determined to transfer all the weight of his influence and power to David's side.

AM I A DOG'S HEAD: This was another way to ask, "Am I a contemptible traitor allied with Judah?" Abner used this opportunity to condemn Ishbosheth and remind him that he would not have been in power at all had Abner not placed him there.

10. TRANSFER THE KINGDOM: Part of Saul's kingdom had already been transferred to David, but Abner now vowed to complete the process by helping David obtain the rest.

12. WHOSE IS THE LAND: Abner implied a conviction that in supporting Ishbosheth he had been going against God's purpose of conferring the sovereignty of the kingdom on David. However, this acknowledgment was no justification of his motives. Abner selfishly wanted to be on the winning side and be honored as the one who brought all the people under David's rule.

13. MICHAL, SAUL'S DAUGHTER: David requested that Michal be brought to him for two reasons. First, it would right the wrong that Saul had committed toward him by having given Michal, who was David's wife, to another man (see 1 Samuel 25:44). Second, it would serve to strengthen David's claim to the throne of all Israel by inclining some of Saul's house to be favorable to his cause.

14. A HUNDRED FORESKINS OF THE PHILISTINES: David reminded Ishbosheth that he had not only paid the dowry to Saul for Michal (one hundred foreskins of the Philistines) but had also delivered double the asking price (see 1 Samuel 18:25–27). Thus, Michal rightfully belonged to him.

16. TO BAHURIM: Located just east of Jerusalem, it became the final location where Paltiel would see Michal, whom Saul had given to him in marriage.

17. ELDERS OF ISRAEL: These men were the recognized leaders of the people. They served as Ishbosheth's advisers and would have been consulted when important decisions needed to be made. Abner stated to them that he

recognized David as the servant of the Lord and that David had the right to the throne according to God's sovereign will.

19. IN THE HEARING OF BENJAMIN: Abner gave special attention to the tribe of Benjamin, because they were Saul's and Ishbosheth's kinsmen.

*A LONG-AWAITED REVENGE: After years of waiting, Joab hatches an evil plot against Abner—and executes it at the city gate.*

21. HE WENT IN PEACE: David made peace with Abner, even though Abner had led the rebellious army against him. David's aim was always to bring peace and unity within Israel, and he was ever ready to forgive those who repented of wrongdoing. Joab was not so forgiving, and it seems he never believed that Abner's change of loyalties was genuine.

22. JOAB CAME FROM A RAID: To gain a balanced picture of Joab, we must remember that he was a great man of valor and served Israel faithfully throughout David's reign. He was one of the generals who led David's army courageously from victory to victory. Still, as we will see in this study and in future events, he was not above performing unscrupulous deeds at times. Joab was faithful to David, but he was also a man of violence.

24. WHAT HAVE YOU DONE: Joab was not shy about confronting David— and his confrontations were often for David's good. In this case, however, he was motivated by a personal vendetta.

25. ABNER . . . CAME TO DECEIVE YOU: This was not true, though it is possible Joab believed it. It is more likely that Joab was trying to manipulate David in order to gain his own revenge.

27. JOAB TOOK HIM ASIDE IN THE GATE: Joab's trick was the ultimate act of treachery. First, the city gate was a location of public debate and justice. As such, it was considered a safe place for disputes to be settled. Second, Hebron itself (where this took place) was one of Israel's cities of refuge—a safe haven for anyone who killed a person accidentally. Joab took advantage of these things to lull Abner into trusting him, and then stabbed him in the belly.

FOR THE BLOOD OF ASAHEL HIS BROTHER: Joab did not have a legitimate grievance against Abner. Abner had killed Asahel in combat—and even then he had tried to avoid doing so.

29. LET IT REST ON THE HEAD OF JOAB: David unfortunately failed to exact justice in his own household. Joab was guilty of murder, and it was

David's responsibility as the king to put him to death. This was a pattern that David would repeat throughout his life.

## UNLEASHING THE TEXT

1) Why did the people of Israel try to make Ishbosheth king instead of David? Why did Abner, Saul's great military leader, side against David?

_____

_____

_____

2) Why did Abner suggest holding a "contest of champions" rather than open battle? Was this a good idea? Why did it fail?

_____

_____

_____

3) What caused Abner to shift his allegiance to David? What was the root cause of the rift that developed between Ishbosheth and Abner?

_____

_____

_____

4) Why did Joab murder Abner? Was Abner deserving of death? Was Joab's anger justified?

_____

_____

_____

_____

## EXPLORING THE MEANING

***Division is the devil's tool.*** The nation of Israel divided when King Saul died, with each faction placing their allegiance behind a different successor to the throne. That same division would return during David's reign and would ultimately divide Israel into two separate nations. Each time the people were divided, strife and civil war resulted.

Satan's goal is to divide God's people, because he knows that if we are busy contending against one another, we won't be doing battle against his forces of darkness. The evil one loves to see us bickering and scratching at one another, and he will do all he can to cause division and contention within the church. He knows that a united body of believers is a powerful force for advancing God's kingdom on earth.

The Lord wants His people to function as one body, to focus on serving one another, and to care for one another as members of that body. As Paul wrote, "Now I plead with you, brethren, by the name of our Lord Jesus Christ, that you all speak the same thing, and that there be no divisions among you, but that you be perfectly joined together in the same mind and in the same judgment . . . For where there are envy, strife, and divisions among you, are you not carnal and behaving like mere men? For when one says, 'I am of Paul,' and another, 'I am of Apollos,' are you not carnal?" (1 Corinthians 1:10; 3:3–4).

***We must submit to the Lord's chosen leaders.*** The division within Israel came about because some were unwilling to submit themselves to David's authority. They felt that a son of Saul should be the next king, and they set about making it a reality in spite of the fact that God had publicly proclaimed David king through the anointing of Samuel.

The basic mindset of the Israelites was that they knew who should govern better than God did. They thought they had the right to choose their own rulers, but this was actually not true. The Lord is the one who places people in positions of power and authority, and He expects His people to submit themselves to those authorities.

God's Word calls us to be submissive to those in authority, whether in government, at home, in the church, or at the workplace. The Bible says, "Let every soul be subject to the governing authorities. For there is no authority except from God, and the authorities that exist are appointed by God. Therefore whoever resists the authority resists the ordinance of God, and those who resist will bring judgment on themselves" (Romans 13:1–2).

***It is God alone who places people in positions of authority.*** David had to fight to establish his throne in Israel. He faced much opposition, both from outside enemies, such as the Philistines, and from foes within his own nation. He fought boldly and effectively, and eventually he gained victory over those foes. Yet he declared clearly that his throne had been established not by the power of his mighty sword but by the power and will of the Lord God Himself.

Abner initially sided against David and then made his own play for the throne of Israel. Yet ultimately God used him to convince the people who had sided with Ishbosheth that God's chosen ruler over all Israel was David. "May God do so to Abner," he said, "and more also, if I do not do for David as the LORD has sworn to him" (2 Samuel 3:9). God made this move sovereignly in His own timing, and David could not claim it was through his own might.

We do not find our security or success through our own efforts or through the world around us. It is the Lord who establishes us where He wants us. "'Not by might nor by power, but by My Spirit,' says the LORD of hosts" (Zechariah 4:6). We attain success and security by submitting to the Lord's sovereign hand.

## REFLECTING ON THE TEXT

5)  How might the civil war between Judah and the other tribes of Israel have been avoided? What did the war cost the nation of Israel?

_____

_____

_____

_____

6) What motivated the people of Israel to reject David as their king? What was wrong with their thinking?

_____

_____

_____

_____

_____

7) When have you witnessed division among God's people? What were some of the causes for it? What was the result?

_____

_____

_____

_____

_____

8) Do you promote peace and unity or stir up strife and division? In what areas might the Lord be calling you to be more of a peacemaker?

_____

_____

_____

_____

_____

## PERSONAL RESPONSE

9) Where do you find your security? In what ways do you tend to place your faith in your own efforts instead of God's sovereignty?

_____

_____

_____

_____

10) How well do you submit to those in authority in government? How well do you submit to those in authority at work? At church? At home?

_____

_____

_____

_____

# 2

# OBEDIENCE AND BLESSING
## *2 Samuel 6:1–23*

## DRAWING NEAR

Why is it important not only to have good intentions when we do something but also to obey God's commands while we are doing it?

_____

_____

_____

_____

## THE CONTEXT

When the Israelites were leaving Egypt and heading toward the Promised Land, the Lord instructed them to create a movable tabernacle for worship. He was very explicit on all the details of that tabernacle—on its construction, on the materials to be used, and on the many articles to be contained within it. One of those articles was the ark of the covenant, an ornate chest containing the tablets of the Law and other sacred objects. On top of the ark were two cherubim, which were carved representations of angels bowed low with their wingtips touching. This ark was the symbol of God's presence among His people.

The Lord also gave explicit instructions on how the ark was to be transported. The craftsmen had created two rings on each of its sides through which long wooden poles were inserted for carrying. Only the Levites (priests from the tribe of Levi) were permitted to move the ark, and they were to balance the wooden poles on their shoulders with the ark in the middle. Nobody was permitted to touch the sacred object at any time, because it represented the physical presence of God. God cannot tolerate sin in His presence.

Before the time Saul was appointed as Israel's first king, the people had foolishly carried the ark into battle against the Philistines. They correctly understood the Lord was the one who fought their battle, but they wrongly assumed the ark would guarantee them victory. God showed them the error in their thinking when He allowed the Philistines to capture the ark. The Philistines carried it back to one of their cities and placed it at the feet of their god Dagon. This was their way of demonstrating that Dagon had defeated the God of Israel, but the Lord let them know they were wrong. Disease and death soon swept through their cities.

The Philistines quickly determined to return the ark to Israel, but they had no knowledge of God's instructions on how to move it. So they just placed it on an oxcart and sent it away. It eventually ended up in the town of Kirjath Jearim, where it remained for many years. Once David was established as the sole ruler of Israel, he decided the time was right to bring the ark back to Jerusalem. However, as he would learn, God demands that His people fully obey His instructions. There are no excuses for violating God's holiness.

## Keys to the Text

Read 2 Samuel 6:1–23, noting the key words and phrases indicated below.

REMEMBERING THE ARK: *The ark of the covenant belonged in Jerusalem, but it had been in Kirjath Jearim for many years. David decides it is time to bring it back.*

6:1. DAVID GATHERED ALL THE CHOICE MEN OF ISRAEL: Ishbosheth lost heart once Abner was dead, and he ultimately was slain by two captains of his troops. This led the rest of Israel to anoint David as their king. David went on to take Jerusalem from the Jebusites and then defeat the Philistines in battle. Once peace had returned to the land, he determined it was time for the ark to return to Jersualem. However, his desire to move the ark surrounded by the most prominent people of Israel, rather than by using Levites, was in direct disobedience to the Lord's commands for moving it. According to 1 Chronicles 13:4, the choice to use prominent men was made because it was thought to be "right in the eyes of all the people."

2. Baale Judah: Literally "lords of Judah." Also known as Kirjath Jearim, it was located about ten miles west of Jerusalem. After the Philistines captured the ark of the covenant, they returned it to the Israelite town of Beth Shemesh. From there the ark was taken to this town.

Lord of Hosts: The word *hosts* can refer to human armies (see Exodus 7:4), celestial bodies (see Deuteronomy 4:19), or heavenly creatures (see Joshua 5:14). This title emphasizes the Lord as sovereign over all of the powers in heaven and on earth, and especially over the armies of Israel.

who dwells between the cherubim: The ark featured two sculptured angels, or cherubim, seated on its top. The Lord was said to dwell between the cherubim because the ark itself represented His presence in Israel.

*Imitating the Philistines: The people disregard God's clear instructions on how to carry the ark and place it instead on an oxcart. It is a technique they learned from the Philistines.*

3. a new cart: The ark was to be moved only by descendants of Kohath, members of the tribe of Levi (see Numbers 3:30–31), and they were to carry it on poles designed for that purpose (see Exodus 25:12–14). The Philistines, however, had returned the ark to Israel by oxcart. David was evidently imitating their example.

house of Abinadab: The man to whom the ark of the Lord had been entrusted after the Philistines returned it to Israel. Uzzah and Ahio were descendants of Abinadab (possibly his grandsons).

5. the house of Israel played music before the Lord: Literally, they "made merry" before the Lord. The entire event had ended up being more of a parade than an act of worship. Thousands of Israelites had lined the street, while those politically connected to David (rather than the priests) surrounded the ark. The return of the ark to Jerusalem, where it belonged, was to be a joyous event for the people of Israel—and it undoubtedly would have been, if they had simply followed the Lord's directions on how to move it.

6. **TOOK HOLD OF IT:** Uzzah's motivation for grabbing the ark was good—the oxen stumbled, and the ark was tottering on the cart. But man's good intentions do not excuse disobedience to God's Word. The sad fact is that David's failure to lead the people according to God's directions caused an innocent man to lose his life.

7. **GOD STRUCK HIM THERE FOR HIS ERROR:** God had clearly warned the people they were not permitted to touch the ark or any of the holy things in the tabernacle, lest they be struck dead (see Numbers 4:15). Not even the high priest was exempt from following these instructions.

8. **DAVID BECAME ANGRY:** God's anger was aroused by man's sinful presumption in disregarding His clear commands, but David's anger was aroused by God's justice. In truth, David's anger was likely directed at himself, because the calamity had come about as a result of his own carelessness.

**PEREZ UZZAH:** The name literally means "outbreak against Uzzah."

9. **DAVID WAS AFRAID OF THE LORD:** There is a "fear of the Lord" that represents healthy respect for His character and holiness, and the fear of God's justice and wrath can move a person toward repentance of sin and salvation. Yet Christians have been saved from the wrath of God, and we should never be afraid to enter His presence. When we do sin, we should not tremble in fear of God's punishment but immediately confess the sin and restore our relationship with Him (see 1 John 1:9). David's fear here was brought about by his own sin. Rather than trembling, he should have confessed it and set about carrying the ark back to Jerusalem in the correct manner.

> **OBEYING GOD'S WORD:** *The people set out to return the ark a second time, but this time they do it in the manner that God has commanded.*

10. **DAVID WOULD NOT MOVE THE ARK:** David, fearing more death and calamity might come on him and the people, was now confused as to whether to carry on the transportation of the ark to Jerusalem. Unconfessed sin can freeze people in their tracks and hinder their continued ministry for the Lord. David would not resume this good task until he had dealt with his guilt.

**OBED-EDOM THE GITTITE:** Literally "servant of Edom." The term *Gittite* can refer to someone from the Philistine city of Gath, but here it is better to see the term related to Gath Rimmon, one of the Levitical cities (see Joshua 21:24–25).

11. THE LORD BLESSED OBED-EDOM AND ALL HIS HOUSEHOLD: Apparently Obed-Edom feared God and honored Him by honoring the ark. God responded by blessing his household.

12. SO DAVID WENT AND BROUGHT UP THE ARK: When David was told that the Lord had blessed the household of Obed-Edom, he recognized God did not desire to rain down judgment and wrath on His people—He desired to bless them. It is important for us to remember this, as it can help us to be quick in confessing sin and restoring our relationship with the Lord. Once David had remembered the love of God, he was quick to restore the ark with gladness.

13. THOSE BEARING THE ARK: This time, the people of Israel carried the ark in the correct manner, bearing it on the shoulders of the Levites rather than trundling it along in an oxcart.

HAD GONE SIX PACES: The sacrifice of the oxen and fatted sheep took place after the first six steps, not after every six steps.

DANCING BEFORE THE LORD: David leads the people into Jerusalem, dancing with joy in the presence of the Lord. His wife Michal, however, is not pleased.

14. DAVID DANCED BEFORE THE LORD: The Hebrews, like other ancient and modern people, had their physical expressions of religious joy as they praised God. In this case, the people were overjoyed that the ark would finally be restored to its rightful place in Jerusalem. David's dancing was an expression of joy in the presence of the Lord and His ark, and he expressed that joy with all his might. As the psalmist would write, "Praise Him with the timbrel and dance; praise Him with stringed instruments and flutes!" (Psalm 150:4).

LINEN EPHOD: A close-fitting, sleeveless outer vest that extended to the hips. The priests wore this garment, especially when officiating before the altar (see Exodus 28:6–14).

16. MICHAL . . . LOOKED THROUGH A WINDOW: Michal was the daughter of Saul and David's first wife. Saul had given her in marriage to David after he slew two hundred Philistines.

SHE DESPISED HIM IN HER HEART: Michal did not share David's over-whelming joy at being in God's presence. She evidently considered David's un-bridled, joyful dancing as conduct unbefitting the dignity and gravity of a king because it exposed him in some ways.

17. IN THE MIDST OF THE TABERNACLE: David had made a tent for the ark of the covenant until a permanent building for it could be built. The song of dedication in Psalm 30 could possibly refer to this tent or to David's own home.

18. HE BLESSED THE PEOPLE IN THE NAME OF THE LORD OF HOSTS: Notice the repetition of David's words, as he blessed the people and then re-turned to bless his own household. Earlier he had been filled with fear in the presence of God, but once he resumed his obedience to the Lord's commands, his fear turned to blessing. Obedience to God always brings great blessings, and those blessings overflow to others.

20. BLESS HIS HOUSEHOLD: David desired the same inevitable success from the Lord as the household of Obed-Edom had experienced. Michal's atti-tude aborted the blessing at that time, but the Lord would bless David's house in the future.

UNCOVERING HIMSELF: In fact, David did not expose himself in any in-decent manner. Michal evidently was appalled to see the king dancing with joy, wearing the ephod—the humble clothes of a priest—rather than elegant royal robes. She felt that David had somehow debased himself with his open expression of joy and worship.

21. IT WAS BEFORE THE LORD: David responded to Michal's accusation by pointing out that he was dancing not for the benefit of the people around him but for the glory of God. It was an act of worship for him, not a public display.

22. I WILL BE EVEN MORE UNDIGNIFIED THAN THIS: David was not concerned about his public image or about appearing dignified and aloof as king. He saw himself through the eyes of God, and that kept him humble in his own sight.

23. MICHAL . . . HAD NO CHILDREN: It is unclear whether this came about because David ceased to have marital relations with Michal or because the Lord disciplined her for her contempt. In Old Testament times, it was con-sidered a reproach to be childless (see 1 Samuel 1:5–6). Michal's childlessness prevented her from providing a successor to David's throne from the family of Saul.

## UNLEASHING THE TEXT

1)  Why did David choose prominent people to move the ark? Why didn't he use Levites? Why do you think he chose to use an oxcart in the first place?

_____

_____

_____

2)  Why did God strike down Uzzah? If you had been Uzzah, what would you have done when you saw the ark teetering on the oxcart?

_____

_____

_____

3)  Compare the two attempts at moving the ark. What was different? What was the same?

_____

_____

_____

4)  Why did Michal become angry with David? If you had been in her position, how would you have responded to the king's dancing?

_____

_____

_____

## Exploring the Meaning

**God is to be worshiped in His prescribed way.** The Lord had given strict instructions to Israel on how to carry the ark. They were to transport it on long poles balanced on their shoulders. No one was allowed to touch it, because it represented the presence of a holy God who cannot tolerate sin. But instead, the people carried the ark in the same manner as the Philistines had done. Unlike the Philistines, however, they knew the commands of God and did not need to invent methods based on what they thought would please a deity.

The Lord not only said *how* the ark was supposed to be moved but also *who* was supposed to move it. He had appointed a particular family of Levites to oversee the ark's transportation. When David first tried to move the ark, he disobeyed this directive and replaced the Levite priests with the prominent political leaders of Israel. With happy music playing (which drew further attention to the blatant disobedience of God's commands), the whole event became a parade. The people of Israel knew better. They had the Word of God to lead them, and they were accountable to obey it.

God cannot be worshiped using whatever means are most appealing or acceptable to the world. In John 4:24, Jesus says those who worship God must "worship in spirit and in truth." As God's people, we must not worship simply by external conformity to religious rituals. Rather, we must worship based on the truth of God's Word and with a Spirit that longs to obey His commands. If the proper heart attitude is absent, worship is false.

**The Lord is eager to bless, not to punish.** David was filled with fear of God's anger when he failed to follow the Lord's prescribed method of carrying the ark, and that fear hindered his ministry. But the Lord was not looking for excuses to display His wrath. Rather, He was eager to bless the people and lead them into righteousness and obedience. He poured out blessings upon the household of Obed-Edom just as He longed to do for the entire nation of Israel.

Our sin can cause us to have an inaccurate perspective of God's character. We can fall into the error of thinking that God is an angry being who looks for shortcomings and failures in the lives of His people and then eagerly punishes and rebukes them for it. The truth is just the opposite. The Lord *longs* to bless His people, and He is always looking for ways to demonstrate His love toward us.

The ultimate example of this is found in Christ. If God had been eager to punish us, He might have simply condemned the entire human race to eternal punishment, since that is precisely what our sins deserved. But instead God sent His own Son to die on the cross to pay the penalty for those sins and enabled us to be restored to fellowship with Him. As David himself wrote, "The LORD is merciful and gracious, slow to anger, and abounding in mercy. He will not always strive with us, nor will He keep His anger forever. He has not dealt with us according to our sins, nor punished us according to our iniquities" (Psalm 103:8–10).

***It's good for us to pour out our worship before the Lord.*** David danced before the Lord, leaping and whirling in an open expression of joy. He was the king of Israel, one of the most powerful leaders in the world at the time, and his position certainly required times of sober dignity. Yet he was also the leader of God's people, and it was in that capacity that he led them in a joyful demonstration of their love for God.

The people had good reason for such joy. They were bringing the ark back to Jerusalem, and the ark itself represented a symbol of the fact that the Creator of the universe had chosen to make His dwelling among them. Of course, the ark was just a *symbol* of God's presence. He did not physically dwell in it, and the people were restricted in their intimacy with God. Christians today have something much more precious: we have the Holy Spirit of God dwelling *inside* us, and nothing could be more intimate than that!

We have good reason for rejoicing as believers in Christ Jesus, for we have intimate access to the presence of God at all times. We should be quick to emulate David's example, expressing our joy before the Lord in blissful praise and worship. As the apostle Paul wrote, "Be filled with the Spirit, speaking to one another in psalms and hymns and spiritual songs, singing and making melody in your heart to the Lord, giving thanks always for all things to God the Father in the name of our Lord Jesus Christ" (Ephesians 5:18–20).

## Reflecting on the Text

5) What does this story told in 2 Samuel 6 reveal about the character of God? What does it reveal about the importance of obedience?

_____

_____

_____

_____

6) How did you react when you read of God's punishment on Uzzah? How did David react? What do our human responses reveal about our understanding of God's Word?

_____

_____

_____

_____

7) To what extent was David responsible for the death of Uzzah? To what extent was Uzzah responsible? How might the tragedy have been avoided?

_____

_____

_____

_____

8) Why did the Israelites imitate the Philistines' method for moving the ark? Why is imitation more appealing to some people than conforming to God's Word?

_____

_____

_____

## PERSONAL RESPONSE

9) Do you tend to view God as eager to punish or eager to bless? How does a person's view of God affect his or her behavior?

_____

_____

_____

10) What are some reasons for rejoicing in your own life? Spend some time today in praise and worship to the Lord.

_____

_____

_____

# 3

# A Throne Established Forever
## *2 Samuel 7:1–29*

## Drawing Near

Why is it critical for us to wait on God's timing when we do something—even if it obviously seems to us to be the right course of action?

_____

_____

_____

## The Context

As David settled into his kingship over Israel, most of his rule was characterized by conflict and warfare. The Israelites had many enemies who persisted in trying to conquer them—and some even wanted to wipe them off the map. The Philistines were one of their most dangerous enemies, and David spent the majority of his reign trying to overthrow their tyranny. In addition to foreign enemies, David also faced multiple rebellions from the Israelites themselves.

Despite this continual opposition to his rule, David never lost sight of the fact that all of his blessings had come from God. He longed to do something in return to demonstrate his love and gratitude for the Lord. In this frame of mind, David got the idea of building a beautiful temple in which the people of Israel could worship God.

As we discussed in the last study, the Lord had commanded the people to construct a portable tabernacle during their exodus from Egypt. This structure was made of cloth and animal skins and was designed to be set up and taken down easily as the people moved from place to place in the wilderness. The tabernacle housed the ark of the covenant, which was the nation's symbol of God's presence. The tabernacle itself was the figurative "dwelling place" of God among His people.

But now, with Israel's wilderness wanderings long since completed, David felt it was not right that he should live in a beautiful palace while God continued to dwell in a portable tent. So he devised a plan to build the temple. The idea itself was not wrong, and God would indeed lead another king to build a temple—but not David. Nevertheless, the Lord blessed David immensely for the love behind his desire to build a permanent dwelling place for the Almighty.

## KEYS TO THE TEXT

Read 2 Samuel 7:1–29, noting the key words and phrases indicated below.

> *A DWELLING PLACE FOR GOD: As time passes in David's reign, he reflects on the fact that he lives in a palace while God's tabernacle is merely a tent. He decides to correct this problem.*

1. WHEN THE KING WAS DWELLING IN HIS HOUSE: David had built his palace with help from Hiram of Tyre. Since Hiram did not become king of Tyre until around 980 BC, the events narrated in this chapter occurred during the last decade of David's reign. By this time the ark of the covenant had been residing in Kirjath Jearim for many years.

THE LORD HAD GIVEN HIM REST FROM ALL HIS ENEMIES: By this point in David's reign, he had conquered all the nations around Israel.

2. THE ARK OF GOD DWELLS INSIDE TENT CURTAINS: The proper place for the ark of the covenant was inside the Holiest of Holies in the tabernacle, which was an area separated from the rest of the tabernacle (and later, the temple) by heavy curtains. David's concern was motivated by humility

and gratitude—it didn't seem right that he should be living in a palace, placed there by God's gracious hand, while God Himself dwelt in a tent. David, of course, was not suggesting that the tabernacle or any other structure could contain the physical presence of God, but he was recognizing that the tabernacle represented God's presence with His people. David just wanted Him to be better represented.

3. NATHAN: Nathan, mentioned here for the first time, was a prophet who was closely associated with David as one of his advisers. He would later confront the king with a far less pleasant message (see 2 Samuel 12), and then upset a plot to usurp the throne from David's son Solomon (see 1 Kings 1).

DO ALL THAT IS IN YOUR HEART: David's intentions were noble, and there was no question that the Lord had been with him in his reign. But apparently neither Nathan nor David consulted the Lord on these plans, which is an oversight that generally leads to errors. The Lord prevented David from doing anything amiss, but that's not always the case. It is important—and always wise—to seek God's counsel before undertaking any new plans.

*GOD SPEAKS TO NATHAN: David and Nathan have rushed forward in their plans without consulting God. Now God has His say in the matter.*

5. MY SERVANT DAVID: The Lord's description of David as "My servant" indicates that David had made obedience to God a top priority in his life. He did not refer to King Saul, David's predecessor, in that same way.

WOULD YOU BUILD A HOUSE FOR ME TO DWELL: God's response to David's plans came in the form of two questions, both of which pertained to building a temple for Him. In this first question, He asked if David was the one who should build the temple—with the expectation of a negative answer (see 1 Chronicles 17:4). According to 1 Chronicles 22:8 and 28:3, God did not choose David to build the temple because he was a warrior who had shed much blood.

7. WHEREVER I HAVE MOVED ABOUT WITH ALL THE CHILDREN OF ISRAEL: God reminded David that His presence had been with the people of Israel throughout their wilderness wanderings and into the Promised Land. As a symbol of His abiding presence, He had been the one to command the people to construct a movable tabernacle that could be assembled and disassembled as the nation moved from place to place.

Why have you not built Me a house: With this second question, God asked if He had ever commanded any leader of His people to build a temple for the ark. In this, He also expected a negative answer. So, contrary to Nathan's and David's intentions and assumptions, God did not want a house at that time and did not want David to build one.

8. I took you from the sheepfold: David was the youngest son of Jesse and had spent his youth tending his father's sheep. Shepherding was one of the lowliest occupations in David's day, and his background would have been considered very humble. Yet the Lord had used his experiences as a shepherd to prepare him for his kingship. David had singlehandedly killed a lion and a bear using the most rudimentary weapons—which set him in good stead to kill Goliath. He had also likely developed his skill as a musician and poet during those years, which enabled him to write many of the psalms. Perhaps most important, however, was the humbleness of his background, which helped him to remember that his position as king was due solely to the Lord's grace and kindness.

9. cut off all your enemies: David faced a great many enemies during his early years as king and the time prior to taking the throne. The Lord had given him victory after victory over those who sought his destruction, but the process had involved much shedding of blood. It was indeed the Lord's will that David defeat Israel's enemies, but He wanted His temple to be constructed by a man whose hands were not sullied with blood.

10. the sons of wickedness: The neighboring nations in Canaan had plagued Israel ever since they entered the Promised Land under Joshua's leadership. God had chosen David to subdue Israel's enemies as well as shepherd His people toward becoming a nation that was not divided by schisms and bids for power. David's job, then, was to unite and strengthen God's people—to care for them as he had once cared for his father's sheep. The job of building a permanent temple would fall to his descendants.

11. I commanded judges: God reminded David that he had raised up a series of judges to lead His people after they had entered into the Promised Land. Eventually, the people had rebelled against that form of government.

*God Blesses David: The Lord pronounces some profound blessings on David and his descendants—and promises the coming Messiah.*

11. The Lord tells you that He will make you a house: David wanted to build a "house" (a temple) for the Lord, but instead the Lord

said He would build a "house" (a dynasty) for David. With these words the Lord established the "Davidic covenant," which represented His unconditional promise to David and his descendants. This was the fourth of five irrevocable and unconditional covenants that God made in the Bible, the first three being the Noahic covenant (see Genesis 9:8–17), the Abrahamic covenant (see 15:12–21), and the priestly covenant (see Numbers 3:1–18; 18:1–20; 25:10–13). The fifth covenant, which actually provided redemption, would later be revealed through the prophet Jeremiah (see 31:31–34) and accomplished by the death and resurrection of Jesus Christ.

12. I WILL ESTABLISH HIS KINGDOM: In the next few verses, the Lord would make promises to David that would have a dual fulfillment. They were fulfilled in the short-term through David's son Solomon, but they were (and will be) fulfilled in the larger, eternal sense through the Son of David, Jesus Christ. The ultimate realization of these promises is found only in Jesus, whose throne will literally be established forever.

14. HE SHALL BE MY SON: David could not have understood how this promise would be literally fulfilled in Jesus, the only begotten Son of God (see Hebrews 1:5). In Semitic thought, the son had the full character of the father, so the future seed of David would have the same essence of God. That Jesus Christ was God incarnate is the central theme of John's gospel.

IF HE COMMITS INIQUITY: As a human father disciplines his sons, so the Lord would discipline the seed of David if he committed iniquity. This refers to the intermediary seed until the Messiah's arrival (any king of David's line from Solomon on), and it is clear from the books of Samuel and Kings that there were many iniquities to correct. However, the ultimate Seed of David would not be a sinner like David's descendants, for he "committed no sin, nor was deceit found in His mouth" (1 Peter 2:22). Significantly, the account of this event told in 1 Chronicles 17, which focused more directly on the Messiah, did not include this statement.

15. MY MERCY SHALL NOT DEPART FROM HIM: This was an expression of the unconditional character of the Davidic covenant. The Messiah would come to His glorious and eternal kingdom, and that promise would not change.

16. YOUR THRONE SHALL BE ESTABLISHED FOREVER: This promise was fulfilled in the person of Jesus Christ, of whom Luke wrote, "He will be great, and will be called the Son of the Highest; and the Lord God will give Him the throne of His father David. And He will reign over the house of Jacob

forever, and of His kingdom there will be no end" (Luke 1:32–33). The word *forever* conveys the idea of an indeterminately long time or into eternity future. It does not mean that there cannot be interruptions, but rather that the outcome is guaranteed. Christ's Davidic reign will conclude human history.

DAVID'S THANKSGIVING: *After Nathan tells David what the Lord has said, the king goes straight to the tabernacle and bows before God in humble adoration.*

**18. SAT BEFORE THE LORD:** David sat before the ark of the covenant in the temporary tent and demonstrated his humble heart in his response to the Lord's promises. He recognized his own lowly origins as a shepherd, but he also understood that no man—regardless of birth or gifts or good deeds—has any right to expect grace and mercy from a holy God. David would later write, "What is man that You are mindful of him, and the son of man that You visit him?" (Psalm 8:4).

**19. A GREAT WHILE TO COME:** David recognized the Lord had spoken about the distant future, not only about his immediate descendant, who would be Solomon.

**IS THIS THE MANNER OF MAN, O LORD GOD:** The *New Living Translation* renders this difficult phrase, "Do you deal with everyone this way, O Sovereign LORD?" However, this statement is better taken as a declaration rather than a question, the idea being that God's covenant promise is for an eternal kingdom, whereby the whole world of man shall be blessed through the coming seed of David. The Davidic covenant was thus a grant that conferred powers, rights, and privileges to David and his seed for the benefit of humankind—which was a promise that left David speechless.

**21. TO MAKE YOUR SERVANT KNOW:** David wisely recognized that the Lord showed His grace and love to humankind solely because He chose to do so—for no person had ever earned God's grace in any way. Today, as in David's time, God shows His true nature to us through His interventions of love, mercy, grace, and justice so all the world might learn of Him. He showered David with blessings both because He loved David and because He wanted the world around him to know that He alone was the one true God.

**23. WHO IS LIKE YOUR PEOPLE, LIKE ISRAEL:** David was here remembering aspects of the Abrahamic covenant (see Genesis 12; 15; 17).

God went to redeem: Here again, David's words had a depth of meaning that he could not have possibly realized. God would one day go forth Himself into the world in the person of Jesus Christ, with the specific purpose of redeeming a holy nation for Himself. That nation would comprise far more than just the people of Israel, for God would make His redemption freely available to the entire human race.

25. the word which You have spoken: David prayed for the fulfillment of the divine promise spoken to him.

28. Your words are true: David accepted by faith that God's words would come true. He had already learned that God always keeps His promises, no matter how impossible they seem at the time.

## Unleashing the Text

1) Why did David want to build a temple for God? What does this reveal about David's character?

_____

_____

_____

_____

_____

2) What did David and Nathan do wrong in their decision to build a temple? What would have been a better approach to the idea?

_____

_____

_____

_____

3) What did God promise to do for David? What covenant did He form with David?

_____

_____

_____

4) What does David's prayer reveal about his attitude toward God's blessings? What does it reveal about his character? About God's character?

_____

_____

_____

## EXPLORING THE MEANING

***God's covenants and promises are fulfilled in Jesus Christ.*** The Lord made many promises to David concerning his own life and the future of his kingdom. He promised that David's son would establish his throne and build a temple, and these promises were fulfilled in Solomon. The Lord had also promised that His people would be planted in the Promised Land—no longer moving about from place to place being harassed by their former enemies—and these oaths were fulfilled in David's lifetime for the people of Israel.

But God's promises went far beyond the lifetimes of David and his son Solomon. God swore that He would establish David's throne and kingdom *forever*, not just for the lifetimes of men. As we have seen, the Lord had made covenants with others before David—such as with Noah and Abraham—but those promises were only partially brought to completion during the lives of the patriarchs.

Jesus is the *complete* fulfillment of God's promises and covenants. All human history has been leading up to God's final redemption of Adam's descendants—the eternal kingdom of God established and ruled over by His Son, Jesus Christ. Jesus is both Son of God and Son of Man, and His human ancestry is traced from the seed of David. David did see God's promises come to pass in his own life, true, but the final fulfillment will come in eternity through Christ.

***The Lord makes His temple in people, not in buildings.*** The pagan nations of David's day believed that the gods looked favorably on those who built the most costly temple in their honor. The more powerful the god, the more majestic the building had to be. So what kind of god, according to such beliefs, would ever dwell inside a portable tent?

Yet this is precisely the form of tabernacle that the Lord commanded the Israelites to create during their exodus from Egypt. God was not concerned with lavish structures built in His honor but with obedient hearts molded by His Word. He selected David to be Israel's king because he had a heart for Himself, not because he would one day want to build a beautiful temple for His sake.

After Christ's resurrection and ascension, God sent His Holy Spirit to dwell in the hearts of His people, making *us* His tabernacles here on earth. As Jesus promised, "I will pray the Father, and He will give you another Helper, that He may abide with you forever—the Spirit of truth, whom the world cannot receive, because it neither sees Him nor knows Him; but you know Him, for He dwells with you and will be in you" (John 14:16–17). Every believer is now a living temple to God. We are, in fact, the most costly "structure" that could ever be dedicated to Him, since He paid for us with His own Son's blood.

***God's dealings with humankind are through His grace, not man's merit.*** Saul was king over Israel prior to David, but his entire reign was characterized by pride. He evidently felt that he had somehow merited being king and could order events as he saw fit. This attitude led him into many grievous sins, including attempts to murder David and consulting a witch for guidance instead of God.

David's life, in contrast, was characterized by humility (with a few significant lapses, as we will see in future studies). As a rule, David recognized he had no merit in himself that deserved God's favor. God promised to establish David's throne forever, and even brought the Messiah into the world through his descendants, but David understood He did these things simply because He chose to do so, not because he had somehow earned God's esteem.

God blesses His people because He loves them, and it is in His very nature to do so. He forgives us because He chooses to forgive, and because His character is forgiving and gracious. No human being can ever earn God's blessings, and no person can ever make atonement for his or her sins. As Paul wrote, "For by grace you have been saved through faith, and that not of yourselves; it is the gift of God, not of works, lest anyone should boast" (Ephesians 2:8–9).

## REFLECTING ON THE TEXT

5) Why did God not want David to build Him a temple? What does this reveal about God's character? What does it reveal about the kingdom of Christ?

_____

_____

_____

6) How do the promises God made to David connect to Christ? What elements of the promises were specifically referring to Jesus? What elements referred to Solomon and other kings?

_____

_____

_____

7) Why did God pour out such blessings on David—even though he and Nathan had failed to seek His guidance concerning the temple? What does this reveal about God's love?

_____

_____

_____

8) What is God's temple on earth today? Why did He choose such a "dwelling place"? What blessings does this bring to God's people?

_____

_____

_____

## PERSONAL RESPONSE

9) What are some specific examples of God's grace that you have seen in your own life?

_____

_____

_____

10) In what ways will you praise God right now for His blessings and grace in your life?

_____

_____

_____

# 4

# Remembering Past Promises
## *2 Samuel 9:1–13*

## Drawing Near

What are some promises you have made to another person? How have you sought to keep those promises even when it was tempting to break them?

_____

_____

_____

## The Context

In David's day, a king's authority was always under the threat of a coup. It seems there was always someone who felt he had a right to the throne, whether by birth or by virtue of some accomplishment. The ruling king had to be constantly on guard, lest the usurper murder him or raise a rebellion against him.

It was not uncommon, therefore, for a king to ferret out any potential competitors and have them put to death. This was especially true when the king had recently taken the throne—and doubly so if, as in David's case, he had himself taken over the throne of another king. Monarchies were passed on from father to son in the ancient world, and Saul's throne would naturally have passed to his son Jonathan after his death. But God had rejected Saul as king and anointed David in his place, so the proper heir to the throne was David.

Nevertheless, as we saw in a previous study, there were those who thought otherwise. No sooner had the tribe of Judah anointed David as king than the other tribes appointed Saul's youngest son, Ishbosheth, as their ruler. Ishbosheth himself was eventually assassinated, but not before the nation had to endure division and civil strife.

In light of all of this, it would have been quite natural for David to want to search for any remaining descendants of Saul who might pose a threat to his authority and the unity of Israel and have them put to death. And David did, in fact, search for Saul's descendants—but not to have them killed. In fact, he not only wanted to let them live but also to honor them and shower them with gifts.

In this study, we will look at the covenant made between David and Jonathan, discover how important it is to keep one's promises, and also witness mercy and grace in action.

## KEYS TO THE TEXT

Read 2 Samuel 9:1–13, noting the key words and phrases indicated below.

*LOOKING FOR WAYS TO BLESS: David has established his throne, and now he searches out any descendants of Saul he can find—but to bless them, not gain revenge against them.*

9:1. NOW DAVID SAID: The events of this chapter in 2 Samuel 9 take place after the writer lists a number of nations that David had subdued—"from Syria, from Moab, from the people of Ammon, from the Philistines, from Amalek, and from the spoil of Hadadezer the son of Rehob, king of Zobah" (2 Samuel 8:12). There was now more stability in the region.

ANYONE WHO IS LEFT OF THE HOUSE OF SAUL: As we have seen, Israel's first king had died by his own hand during a battle against the Philistines. Most of his sons had also died in battle that day, including Jonathan, whom Saul assumed would be his heir.

THAT I MAY SHOW HIM KINDNESS: This phrase might have startled David's listeners. Saul had tried repeatedly to murder David, even though David had always served him faithfully. It would have been predictable for Saul's heirs to attempt to take back the throne, and David could well have decided to take revenge against Saul's descendants for the many years of pain the former king had caused him. A Canaanite king might easily have asked, "Is there anyone left of my former enemy's household *that I may put him to death*?" David's desire to show kindness to the descendants of the man who tried to kill him provides a stunning picture of his godliness.

FOR JONATHAN'S SAKE: Jonathan and David had been intimate friends. Jonathan had helped David escape from the angry Saul, and the two had sworn an oath that David would show kindness to Jonathan and his family when he came to power (see 1 Samuel 20:14–15). David would continue to display loving loyalty toward Jonathan by showing mercy to his descendants.

ZIBA AND MEPHIBOSHETH: *Saul's grandson Mephibosheth had become lame at the time of Saul's death. He is now living far from David, and Saul's steward is running his estate.*

2. ZIBA: This man was evidently the chief steward of Saul's estate. After the deaths of Saul and Jonathan, the estate went to Mephibosheth, who became Ziba's employer.

3. THE KINDNESS OF GOD: It is significant that David considered his oath to Jonathan as a responsibility before God. He also saw it as a reflection of the kindness that God had so often shown to him. By keeping his oath and showing kindness to the house of Saul, David was imitating God.

LAME IN HIS FEET: Mephibosheth was a young boy when Saul and Jonathan died. When news of the death of Saul and Jonathan reached his family, his nurse hastily grabbed him and fled for their lives. In the process, he fell and became lame in both his feet (see 2 Samuel 4:4).

4. MACHIR THE SON OF AMMIEL: He was evidently a man of wealth (see 2 Samuel 17:27–29).

LO DEBAR: A city located in Gilead, east of the Jordan River, about ten miles south of the Sea of Galilee. Mephibosheth might have deliberately situated himself in this town located a safe distance away from the City of David.

6. MEPHIBOSHETH THE SON OF JONATHAN: Mephibosheth would have been only twelve years old at the time of Ishbosheth's death.

*MERCY AND GRACE: Although David might have been expected to put Mephibosheth to death, he grants him life—and much more.*

7. RESTORE TO YOU ALL THE LAND: It was remarkable enough that King David would permit Mephibosheth to remain alive. But David went far beyond showing mercy; he showed him tremendous grace by restoring all the lands and possessions his family had lost when Saul died. It is possible that Saul's lands had been usurped by Ziba himself, as later events will make it clear that something was not quite right in Mephibosheth's household.

YOU SHALL EAT BREAD AT MY TABLE CONTINUALLY: David desired to honor Mephibosheth by bringing him into the royal palace and providing for his daily needs. David's actions toward Mephibosheth paint a picture of God's grace toward sinners. It would have been more than enough if God had merely offered forgiveness for sins, but He went far beyond that by adopting us as His children and inviting us to share freely of His blessings. He even invites us to join Him regularly at His table in the Lord's Supper.

8. DEAD DOG: A dead dog was considered contemptible and useless. Mephibosheth saw himself as such in that he knew he had not merited David's kindness and there was no way for him to repay it. David's offer was an extraordinary expression of grace and beauty to his covenant with Jonathan.

10. WORK THE LAND FOR HIM: It is possible that David spelled out these details for Ziba because Ziba was appropriating Mephibosheth's property for his own gain.

FIFTEEN SONS AND TWENTY SERVANTS: These details on Ziba show he was a man of wealth and power. It also shows that the land given by David was substantial. This wealth would cause problems for both him and Mephibosheth in the future.

12. WHOSE NAME WAS MICHA: This son of Mephibosheth would become the representative of the house of Saul. His numerous offspring would become leading men in the tribe of Benjamin (see 1 Chronicles 8:35–38; 9:41–44).

## GOING DEEPER

In Ephesians 2:1–18, Paul explains how God, through His mercy and grace, sent Jesus to give us life when we deserved death. Read that passage and note the key words and phrases below.

*FROM DEATH TO LIFE: Paul explains the riches of God's grace by painting a picture of our former state, when we belonged to the world, and our current exalted state in Christ.*

2:1. DEAD IN TRESPASSES AND SINS: This is a sobering reminder of the total sinfulness and lostness from which believers have been redeemed. The word *in* indicates the realm or sphere in which unregenerate sinners exist. They are not dead because of the sinful acts they have committed but because of their sinful nature.

2. COURSE OF THIS WORLD: This refers to the world order—that is, humanity's values and standards that are apart from God and Christ. In 2 Corinthians 10:4–5, Paul referred to these ideologies as "fortresses" (NASB) in which people are imprisoned and from which they need to be set free. These ideologies must be brought captive to Christ and obedience to the truth.

THE PRINCE OF THE POWER OF THE AIR: This title refers to Satan. In 2 Corinthians 4:4, Paul also referred to him as "the god of this age."

4. GOD, WHO IS RICH IN MERCY, BECAUSE OF HIS GREAT LOVE: Salvation glorifies God because it puts on display His boundless mercy and love for those who are spiritually dead due to their sinfulness.

5. WHEN WE WERE DEAD . . . MADE US ALIVE: Mephibosheth saw himself as a "dead dog" before David, contemptible and worthless, but David lifted him up and offered him grace and mercy. In the same way, we were spiritually "dead dogs" before God's salvation brought us to life. The power that raised us out of death and made us alive is the same power that energizes every aspect of our Christian living.

6. RAISED US UP TOGETHER, AND MADE US SIT TOGETHER: Just as David raised up Mephibosheth and invited him to sit at his table, so God has raised us up and invited us to join Him at His table (see Song of Songs 2:4). The verb tense Paul uses in this verse for *raised* and *made* indicates these are immediate and direct results of salvation. Not only are believers dead to sin and alive to righteousness through Christ's resurrection, but they also enjoy their Lord's exaltation and share in His preeminent glory.

IN THE HEAVENLY PLACES: This refers to the supernatural realm where God reigns. This spiritual realm is where believers' blessings are, their inheritance is, their affections should be, and where they enjoy fellowship with the

Lord. It is the realm from which all divine revelation has come and where all praise and petitions go.

7. RICHES OF HIS GRACE: God's salvation, of course, is very much for the believer's blessing, but it is even more for the purpose of eternally glorifying God for bestowing on believers His endless and limitless grace and kindness. The whole of heaven glorifies God for what He has done in saving sinners. As John later wrote, "I looked, and behold, a great multitude . . . [were] crying out with a loud voice, saying, 'Salvation belongs to our God who sits on the throne, and to the Lamb!'" (Revelation 7:9–10).

8. FAITH, AND THAT NOT OF YOURSELVES: Paul's words here refer to the entire previous statement of salvation. Although we are required to believe for salvation to occur, even that faith is part of the gift of God that saves us, and we cannot exercise it by our own power. God's grace is preeminent in every aspect of salvation.

10. CREATED IN CHRIST JESUS FOR GOOD WORKS: Our good works cannot produce salvation, but they are subsequent and resultant God-empowered fruits and evidences of it. Like our salvation, God ordained our sanctification and good works before time began.

*BREAKING DOWN WALLS: Paul continues by explaining how Jesus breaks down the walls that separate us from God and brings us the hope of eternal life.*

13. YOU WHO ONCE WERE FAR OFF: This is a common term in rabbinical writings to describe Gentiles, who were apart from the true God.

HAVE BEEN BROUGHT NEAR: Mephibosheth considered himself an outsider, but David brought him near and gave him a place at his own table. In the same way, every person who trusts in Christ alone for salvation—whether Jew or Gentile—is brought into spiritual union and intimacy with God. The atoning work that Jesus accomplished through His death on the cross washes away the penalty of sin and, ultimately, even its presence.

14. HE HIMSELF: This emphatically indicates that Jesus alone is our source of peace. "His name will be called Wonderful, Counselor, Mighty God, Everlasting Father, Prince of Peace" (Isaiah 9:6).

15. ABOLISHED IN HIS FLESH THE ENMITY: Christ, through His death on the cross, abolished the Old Testament ceremonial laws, feasts, and sacrifices

that had separated Jews from Gentiles. However, God did not abolish His moral law—as summarized in the Ten Commandments and written on the hearts of people—but incorporated it into the New Covenant. As Jesus said, "Do not think that I came to destroy the Law or the Prophets. I did not come to destroy but to fulfill. For assuredly, I say to you, till heaven and earth pass away, one jot or one tittle will by no means pass from the law till all is fulfilled" (Matthew 5:17–18).

ONE NEW MAN: Christ does not exclude anyone who comes to Him, and those who are His are not spiritually distinct from one another. The word translated *new* in this verse is from a Greek word that refers to something completely unlike what it was before. It refers to being different in kind and quality.

16. RECONCILE THEM BOTH TO GOD: As Jews and Gentiles are brought to God through Christ Jesus, they are brought together with each other. This was accomplished at the cross when Jesus took God's wrath so divine justice could be satisfied and reconciliation with God could become a reality for those who believe in Him.

17. PREACHED PEACE: The Greek word for *preached* literally means "to bring or announce good news." In the New Testament, it is almost always used of proclaiming the good news that sinners can be reconciled to God through the salvation bought by Jesus Christ. In this context, Christ, the One who Himself is our peace, also announced the good news of peace.

18. ACCESS BY ONE SPIRIT TO THE FATHER: Just as Mephibosheth had no right to demand access to David's presence, sinners have no right within themselves for access to God's presence. However, believers have been granted that right through faith in Christ's sacrificial death. The resources of the Trinity belong to believers the moment they receive Christ. The Holy Spirit presents them before the heavenly throne of God the Father, where they are welcome to come with boldness at any time. (See Hebrews 4:16.)

## UNLEASHING THE TEXT

1) What motivated David to honor Mephibosheth? If you had been in David's place, how do you think you would have acted?

_____

_____

_____

2) If you had been in Mephibosheth's place, what would your reaction have been on being called to the king's court? What would you have expected?

_____

_____

_____

_____

3) What was the difference between the way the kings of pagan nations treated their potential rivals and the way David treated his?

_____

_____

_____

4) What was the significance of David inviting Mephibosheth to sit at his table "like one of the king's sons" (2 Samuel 9:11)?

_____

_____

_____

_____

## Exploring the Meaning

**We must fulfill our promises.** David and Jonathan loved one another like brothers, and either would willingly have laid down his life for the other. In fact, Jonathan did risk his life by protecting David against Saul's murderous plans. The two men swore an oath of friendship, and David promised Jonathan that he would always show kindness to him and his family.

But Jonathan died young, fighting bravely against overwhelming odds with the Philistines. David, on the other hand, became king and had battles of his own to deal with. From the world's perspective, he would have been well within his kingly rights to put Mephibosheth to death so he would not prove a menace to his throne. In the world's eyes, it would have been more than gracious for David to simply ignore Mephibosheth and let him live. But David took his oath and promise to Jonathan seriously. He went beyond what was merely expected and deliberately showed compassion to Jonathan's son.

In this David was imitating the character of God, who always keeps His promises. As God's people, we too should take care to fulfill our word, whether it is given as a solemn oath (as in marriage vows) or a simple promise. To not do so invites divine judgment. In fact, according to James, it is better to not give your word at all than to give it and not keep it. "But above all, my brethren, do not swear, either by heaven or by earth or with any other oath. But let your 'Yes' be 'Yes,' and your 'No,' 'No,' lest you fall into judgment" (James 5:12).

***Do not take revenge.*** David had served King Saul loyally and exceptionally. As a young man, he had boldly faced the giant Goliath when all of Saul's army—and Saul himself—had been afraid to do so. He had later served at Saul's court, calming the king's strange moods with his songs.

Yet Saul had tried many times to murder David. He had thrown a spear at him in his own court, and he had hunted him mercilessly for years. David had demonstrated, even then, that he was loyal to Saul by not hurting him even when he had Saul completely at his mercy. Saul had wronged him, and David had a considerable score to settle—yet he never took revenge into his own hands. Even when David was king and had the perfect right (in the world's eyes) to exact vengeance against Saul's heirs, he refrained—and went beyond, even to the point of showering gifts and honor on Saul's grandson.

It can be hard for us to resist taking revenge on those who have hurt us in the past. Our human nature sees it as simple justice to return evil for evil. But the Lord calls us to the higher standard of acting according to Christ's nature rather than our fallen human nature. In fact, Jesus commands us to go beyond withholding vengeance by returning good for evil, blessing those who curse us and doing good to those who harm us. "I say to you, love your enemies, bless those who curse you, do good to those who hate you, and pray for those who spitefully use you and persecute you, that you may be sons of your Father in heaven" (Matthew 5:44–45).

**God shows us both mercy and grace.** Mercy is the act of withholding judgment on a guilty person. A judge demonstrates mercy when he gives a criminal a second chance or confers a judgment that is less than what the criminal deserves. Grace goes beyond mercy. It is not merely withholding deserved judgment against a person but also bestowing an undeserved gift.

Imagine if a criminal were found guilty of murder, and the judge determined for some reason to withhold the death penalty. That criminal would have received mercy, even if he still faced a stiff jail sentence. But imagine if that judge let the murderer go free from all judgment and even gave him great wealth to start a new life. That criminal would have received both mercy *and* grace, though at the expense of doing justice to the victims of the crime.

God's grace and mercy, however, are perfect. He did not ignore justice when He offered redemption to sinners—our sins brought the death penalty, and that penalty had to be paid. But God set us free from the penalty our sins deserved (mercy), made us heirs with His Son Jesus (grace), and paid for our sins (justice) Himself by giving His Son to die in our stead.

## REFLECTING ON THE TEXT

5) How does David's treatment of Mephibosheth demonstrate the character of God?

_____

_____

_____

6) Why did David go to such lengths to fulfill his promise to Jonathan? What does this teach about the importance of keeping our word?

_____

_____

_____

7) What is the difference between mercy and grace? How has God shown you mercy? How has He shown you grace?

_____

_____

_____

8) When have you shown mercy or grace to someone else? Who is in need of your mercy at this present moment?

_____

_____

_____

## PERSONAL RESPONSE

9) Do you generally keep your word? What promises have you forgotten to fulfill?

_____

_____

_____

10) How do you treat people who mistreat you? What relationships might the Lord want you to improve in this regard?

_____

_____

_____

# THE LIFE OF DAVID

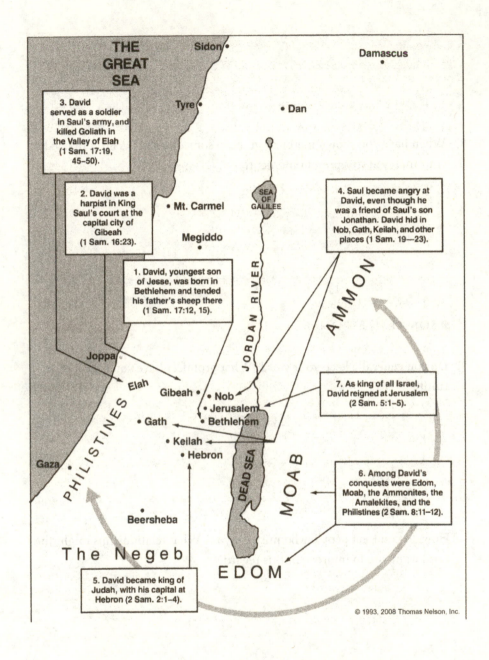

THE GREAT SEA

Sidon

Damascus

3. David served as a soldier in Saul's army, and killed Goliath in the Valley of Elah (1 Sam. 17:19, 45–50).

Tyre

Dan

2. David was a harpist in King Saul's court at the capital city of Gibeah (1 Sam. 16:23).

Mt. Carmel

SEA OF GALILEE

4. Saul became angry at David, even though he was a friend of Saul's son Jonathan. David hid in Nob, Gath, Keilah, and other places (1 Sam. 19—23).

Megiddo

1. David, youngest son of Jesse, was born in Bethlehem and tended his father's sheep there (1 Sam. 17:12, 15).

JORDAN RIVER

AMMON

Joppa

Elah

Gibeah • Nob

7. As king of all Israel, David reigned at Jerusalem (2 Sam. 5:1–5).

PHILISTINES

• Jerusalem

• Gath • Bethlehem

• Keilah

• Hebron

DEAD SEA

MOAB

Gaza

6. Among David's conquests were Edom, Moab, the Ammonites, the Amalekites, and the Philistines (2 Sam. 8:11–12).

Beersheba

The Negeb

EDOM

5. David became king of Judah, with his capital at Hebron (2 Sam. 2:1–4).

© 1993, 2008 Thomas Nelson, Inc.

# 5

# DAVID'S ACTS OF SIN
## *2 Samuel 11:1–27*

## DRAWING NEAR

What are some examples you can think of in which a person being in the wrong place at the wrong time led to disaster?

_____

_____

_____

## THE CONTEXT

After David extended mercy to Mephibosheth, he learned the king of the Ammonites had died. David sent ambassadors to express his condolences as a gesture of goodwill, but this was treated with contempt when the Ammonites disgraced the ambassadors and sent them home in shame. As a result, war broke out between the Ammonites and Israel. Joab led the army in a siege against their city of Rabbah, but David decided to stay at home in his palace.

In those days, the king was responsible to lead his army into battle. David's place during this conflict was on the battlefield with his men, not on the roof of his house taking a nap. We are not told why David chose to not be involved in the fighting, but in some measure he was shirking his responsibilities. This temporary lack of diligence led him into grievous sin.

The houses in David's day had flat roofs, and people would often conduct many mundane activities there. The cool breeze made it a good place for one's daily bathing, and the low wall surrounding the roof afforded an adequate screen from passersby in the street. Thus, a woman was not being immodest if she went on her roof to bathe.

Unfortunately, in this case David's rooftop overlooked that of another; in fact, it overlooked that of a very beautiful woman. David was at home with nothing to do, which certainly contributed to the tragic events that followed. In this sad chapter, we will see how one bad decision on David's part led to another bad decision, and how one seemingly insignificant sin can have disastrous consequences.

## KEYS TO THE TEXT

Read 2 Samuel 11:1–27, noting the key words and phrases indicated below.

*DAVID TAKES A HOLIDAY: Israel is at war with the Ammonites, but David is indulging himself with some time off at home. The king's place, however, is with his army.*

11:1. IN THE SPRING OF THE YEAR: The events in this chapter are thought to have occurred roughly ten years after David established himself in Jerusalem. In the Near East, kings normally went out to battle in the spring of the year because of the good weather and the abundance of food available along the way.

DAVID SENT JOAB: David dispatched Joab, his army commander, with his mercenary soldiers and the army of Israel to continue the battle against the Ammonites that the nation had begun the previous year (see 2 Samuel 10:14).

THEY DESTROYED THE PEOPLE OF AMMON: These events are described in 2 Samuel 10.

BESIEGED RABBAH: The capital of the Ammonites, located about twenty-four miles east of the Jordan River opposite Jericho.

2. DAVID AROSE FROM HIS BED: This was in the late afternoon, not in the middle of the night. David had indulged himself with a nap, probably

on the roof of his house, where he could enjoy the cool breeze. So far David had done nothing overtly sinful, though staying home while his army was at war and napping comfortably suggest he was indulging himself in unnecessary luxuries. Again, such behavior is not inherently wrong, but it can place a person in the way of temptation—as we shall immediately see.

THE DEADLY TRIO: *David awakes from a nap and finds himself confronted with the lust of the eyes, the lust of the flesh, and the pride of life.*

HE SAW A WOMAN BATHING: The roofs of buildings in David's day were level and used frequently for a variety of activities. David's rooftop was higher than the surrounding buildings. His view of Bathsheba bathing was not due to any voyeurism, but seems to be merely accidental.

THE WOMAN WAS VERY BEAUTIFUL TO BEHOLD: Although David's view of Bathsheba was inadvertent, we can discern he allowed his gaze to linger, rather than turning away his head as would have been proper. The first step in David's downward slide was to shirk responsibility—motivated by the pride of his position. His second step was to indulge the lust of the eyes.

3. DAVID SENT AND INQUIRED ABOUT THE WOMAN: Here we have the third step in David's fall: he indulged the lust of the flesh.

IS THIS NOT BATHSHEBA: Bathsheba's name will not be used again until 2 Samuel 12:24. Rather, to intensify the sin of David's adultery, the writer emphasizes she was the wife of Uriah. Later, in the genealogy of Christ found in Matthew, the gospel writer refers to Bathsheba as "her who had been the wife of Uriah" (1:6).

THE DAUGHTER OF ELIAM: The father of Bathsheba was one of David's mighty men (see 2 Samuel 23:34). Eliam was the son of Ahithophel, which means Bathsheba was Ahithophel's granddaughter (see 15:12; 16:15). This could explain why Ahithophel, one of David's counselors, later gave his allegiance to Absalom during his revolt against David.

URIAH THE HITTITE: Uriah was a loyal soldier of David and had earned renown for his deeds of valor. He was also considered one of David's "mighty men" (see 2 Samuel 23:8, 39). Although he was a Hittite, he bore a Hebrew name that meant "the LORD is my light." This indicates that Uriah was a worshiper of the one true God.

4. DAVID SENT MESSENGERS . . . TOOK HER . . . LAY WITH HER: This threefold sequence of sin is reminiscent of Eve in the garden of Eden. "So when the woman *saw* that the tree was good for food, that it was pleasant to the eyes, and a tree desirable to make one wise, she *took* of its fruit and *ate*" (Genesis 3:6, emphasis added). Like Eve, David gazed on what was forbidden and permitted himself to be filled with desire. He then reached, took, and sinned. As a result, his life would never be the same.

SHE WAS CLEANSED FROM HER IMPURITY: This means Bathsheba had completed her menstrual cycle and followed the ceremonial cleansing prescribed by the Law (see Leviticus 15:19–30). This makes it clear she was not pregnant by her husband, Uriah, when she had relations with David.

*DAVID'S COVER-UP: The king suddenly fears that people will learn of his sin, and he tries to cover it up. But he should have been more concerned with the Lord's opinion.*

5. I AM WITH CHILD: The only words of Bathsheba recorded about this incident acknowledge the resultant condition of her sin, which became evident by her pregnancy. The Mosaic law prescribed the death penalty for those who committed adultery—both the man and the woman (see Leviticus 20:10). David's role as king did not place him above God's law; on the contrary, as the leader of God's people, he was all the more accountable for this sin.

6. SEND ME URIAH THE HITTITE: David began this process by shirking his responsibility as commander of Israel's army. Here he openly abused that position of power by arbitrarily calling one of his best fighters home from battle merely to cover his own transgression. This inane conversation was a ploy to get Uriah to come home and sleep with his wife, so it would appear he had fathered the child, thus sparing David the public shame and Bathsheba possible death.

7. DAVID ASKED HOW JOAB WAS DOING: This ridiculous questioning must have seemed peculiar to Uriah. The king could have gained such basic information from any underling and hardly required the perspective of one of his best warriors. Yet there is no record Uriah ever questioned his king's intentions. He was a good soldier, and everything we are told indicates he was also a man of strong character.

8. GO DOWN TO YOUR HOUSE AND WASH YOUR FEET: In David's day this washing was done before going to bed, so the idiom means to "go home

and go to bed." To a soldier coming from the battlefield, it said boldly, "Enjoy your wife sexually." David even sent along a gift of food, intending for Uriah and Bathsheba to enjoy a romantic dinner together. He was obviously hoping that Uriah would take advantage of the furlough to be intimate with his wife.

9. URIAH SLEPT AT THE DOOR OF THE KING'S HOUSE: Uriah wanted to be a loyal example to his soldiers who were still in the field, so he did not take advantage of King David's less-than-honorable offer. It is a natural reflex for us to try to hide our sin and prevent others from discovering it, but this is not what God calls His people to do. Rather, we are to confess our sins and not hide them. David's cover-up failed, as it was God's will to bring his sin to light. As Moses warned the people of Israel, "Be sure your sin will find you out" (Numbers 32:23).

11. THE ARK AND ISRAEL AND JUDAH ARE DWELLING IN TENTS: The ark of the covenant was residing in either the tent in Jerusalem (see 2 Samuel 6:17) or in a tent with the army of Israel on the battlefield (see 1 Samuel 4:6; 14:18). Uriah felt it would be wrong for him to enjoy luxury while God and His people were living in tents. This is just one of the ways in which Uriah unintentionally demonstrated at this point that he was a man of nobler character than David.

SHALL I THEN GO TO MY HOUSE: Uriah had a strong sense of his responsibility. How could he indulge himself in the comforts of home while his fellow soldiers were out fighting in battle? He understood his place was with the army, which provides a strong contrast to David's self-indulgence.

13. HE MADE HIM DRUNK: David did not give up. He thought Uriah might loosen his standards and self-discipline if only he had some alcohol in him. Notice how David's sin and cover-up caused him to lead others into sin.

*DAVID COMMITS MURDER: The cover-up has failed, thanks to Uriah's loyal character, so David resorts to the next expedient. He orders Uriah's death.*

14. SENT IT BY THE HAND OF URIAH: This reveals the ugliness of sin. David had committed adultery with the wife of one of his most loyal followers and had further used Uriah's loyalty in an attempt to cover his own sin. Now he abused Uriah's trust by having him deliver the order commanding his own murder.

15. THAT HE MAY BE STRUCK DOWN AND DIE: David thought that if Uriah were dead, people would assume Bathsheba was carrying Uriah's child. In this way, David engaged in another crime deserving of capital punishment (see Leviticus 24:17). His plan worked for a time. It is important to note that David's sin of lust led to the sin of adultery, which led to the sin of cover-up and abuse of power, which finally led to the sin of murder. Sin breeds more sin, and the only way to stop the destructive cycle is to repent and confess our sins.

17. THE SERVANTS OF DAVID FELL: As Joab revealed in his message to the king (see verse 21), this sortie was probably motivated by David's order for Uriah's death. Joab probably would not have sent his men against the fortified city at this point, for he knew he would suffer large casualties. Here again we see that David's sin affected many innocent lives.

18. JOAB SENT AND TOLD DAVID ALL THE THINGS CONCERNING THE WAR: Joab sent a man with a veiled message to tell David that his wish had been carried out. Joab must have known the reason behind this military deployment.

21. A WOMAN WHO CAST A PIECE OF A MILLSTONE: This is a reference to the story told in Judges 9:52–53: "So Abimelech came as far as the tower and fought against it; and he drew near the door of the tower to burn it with fire. But a certain woman dropped an upper millstone on Abimelech's head and crushed his skull."

URIAH THE HITTITE IS DEAD ALSO: Joab was absolving himself of any responsibility for Uriah's death—and also for poor military leadership. He was subtly reminding David that he was merely following the king's orders. It is also a tragic commentary that he referred to Uriah as "your servant Uriah." David had indeed betrayed one of his most loyal soldiers.

> GOD IS NOT MOCKED: *David's attempt at a cover-up seems to have worked, and he hardens his heart to his own guilt. But God is not finished with the matter.*

25. DO NOT LET THIS THING DISPLEASE YOU: The final step in David's cycle of sin was that he became hardened to his own guilt, and he urged others to join in hardening their hearts as well. When we indulge our sinful desires, we gradually harden our hearts to the Lord's convictions, searing our consciences to the point we no longer feel any guilt over sin.

SO ENCOURAGE HIM: David hypocritically expressed indifference to those who died. He consoled Joab and authorized him to continue the attack against Rabbah.

26. SHE MOURNED FOR HER HUSBAND: The customary period of mourning was probably seven days (see Genesis 50:10; 1 Samuel 31:13). It is interesting there is no mention of David mourning; he had not yet repented of his sins.

27. THE THING THAT DAVID HAD DONE DISPLEASED THE LORD: Literally, "was evil in the eyes of the LORD." This is an ominous ending to this passage. David had successfully covered up his sins and hidden them from the eyes of men, but it was impossible for him to cover his sins from the eyes of God. The effects of David's wrongdoing would be far-reaching and profound.

## UNLEASHING THE TEXT

1) What led David to be tempted by sin? What might he have done to avoid the temptation?

_____

_____

_____

2) How did David's sin multiply? What are the different sins that David committed?

_____

_____

_____

3) What steps did David take to cover up his sin? Why did his first plans fail?

_____

_____

_____

4) How are Uriah and David different in this passage? How are they similar?

_____

_____

_____

## EXPLORING THE MEANING

**The Lord calls us to confess our sins.** David slipped into a downward spiral of sin, beginning with self-indulgence and leading to his adultery with Bathsheba. His immediate concern seemed to be that people would find out what he had done, but he should have been more concerned with how it would affect his relationship with God. This misdirected fear led him to attempt a cover-up, as if the worst thing that could come as a result of his sin was that someone might find out. It did not occur to him that the Lord saw, and the Lord was displeased.

In our next study, we will see that David eventually did confess his sin and repent before the Lord, and the Lord forgave him and restored him to fellowship. But it would have been far better if he had repented immediately, and better still if he had not committed the sin in the first place. His attempts to cover his transgressions led to more sin and caused increased suffering for others around him.

God wants His people to refrain from sinful behavior, but He also knows that we are sinners by birth. Being born again into the family of Christ does not mean we will never sin again. As John writes, "If we say that we have no sin, we deceive ourselves, and the truth is not in us" (1 John 1:8). We *will* sin, but when we do, the Lord calls us to confess and repent immediately and not try to conceal it. "If we confess our sins, He is faithful and just to forgive us our sins and to cleanse us from all unrighteousness" (verse 9). Confession leads to forgiveness and reconciliation, but cover-up leads to further sin and suffering.

**Sin breeds more sin.** David's problems began when he indulged his flesh and avoided the responsibilities of leading his army in battle. This led to a temptation he would have most likely avoided otherwise. He sinned openly when he gazed on Bathsheba during her bath, which inflamed his lust. This lust led to the sin of sexual immorality with a woman who was not his wife, which led him to err further by trying to hide his guilt from the people around him. And this sin led to the sin of murder.

It is important to understand that David alone was responsible for this tragic sequence of sin. The book of James bears this out: "Let no one say when he is tempted, 'I am tempted by God'; for God cannot be tempted by evil, nor does He Himself tempt anyone. But each one is tempted when he is drawn away by *his own* desires and enticed. Then, when desire has conceived, it gives birth to sin; and sin, when it is full-grown, brings forth *death*" (1:13–15, emphasis added). David made one bad decision, which led to another bad decision, and another—and the end result was the death of many innocent men.

Like David, we can find ourselves in a downward spiral of sin when we indulge our fleshly desires. The good news, however, is that God offers grace to cover our sin and the Holy Spirit to convict us of sin—and to help us avoid it in the first place.

*Faithfulness to our responsibilities can protect us from disaster.* David could likely have avoided this tragic failure if he had remained faithful in his responsibilities. The role of the king was to lead the army in battle, and his place was on the battlefield with Joab—not receiving reports of the distant conflict while he sat comfortably at home. Uriah, on the other hand, presents a startling contrast in this regard. He never lost sight of his responsibilities as a soldier and a servant of the king, and this faithfulness inadvertently foiled David's intended cover-up.

The story of Joseph, told in Genesis 37–41, gives us an example of how faithfulness cannot only protect us but also bring with it great blessings. Joseph was a mere slave in the house of Potiphar, yet he was faithful to his master and diligent in his duties. This faithfulness led to him being falsely accused of adultery with his master's wife, and he found himself in prison for a crime he didn't commit. Yet even there he remained faithful to the small tasks the Lord gave him, and his faithfulness ultimately led him to a position of authority over all Egypt.

At times our responsibilities can seem small and insignificant, and it can be easy for us to justify shirking them, just as David did. However, when we avoid our responsibilities, we often set ourselves up for sin. On the other hand, when we are faithful to our responsibilities, the Lord often blesses that faithfulness.

## REFLECTING ON THE TEXT

5) Why did David try to cover his sin? What motivated the cover-up?

_____

_____

_____

6) Who suffered due to David's sin? Why do the innocent often suffer as a result of other people's sins?

_____

_____

_____

7) Why is there no reference to God's view of David's actions until the final verse of 2 Samuel 11? What does that teach us about David's thinking? Why do you think David never sought the Lord during this time?

_____

_____

_____

8) Describe the following sins in your own words, and give examples for each.

Lust of the flesh:

_____

_____

_____

Lust of the eyes:

_____

_____

_____

Pride of life:

_____

_____

_____

## PERSONAL RESPONSE

9) How faithful are you to the responsibilities God has given you? In what areas do you need to be more diligent?

_____

_____

_____

10) Is there any sin in your life that you are trying to cover up? Take time right now to confess it before the Lord.

_____

_____

_____

# 6

# DAVID'S SINS ARE REVEALED
## 2 Samuel 12:1–25

## DRAWING NEAR

Why do you think those in positions of authority are often reluctant to admit their mistakes? How does our society tend to view those who are willing to admit their errors in judgment?

_____

_____

_____

## THE CONTEXT

As this study opens, time has passed since David's sins of adultery and murder. He has married Bathsheba, and she has borne him a son. Yet even now David has not repented of his sins, and he apparently feels he has successfully covered them up. The people in his court, as far as we know, are unaware of what David has done, or at least they have said nothing of the matter.

But God *is* aware, and He is not content to pretend that nothing wrong has been done. David thought he could cover his sin because he was viewing it from the perspective of the world—as long as nobody gets upset, there's no problem. God's perspective, however, is vastly different. David's sin has damaged his relationship with the Lord, and God will not permit that situation to go unresolved.

In this study we will meet the prophet Nathan once again, but this time his conversation with David is not as pleasant as it was when he spoke of God's covenant with his house. This time, God has sent Nathan to confront the king with his grievous sins and lead him to confess and repent before the Lord. Nathan's approach to the confrontation is interesting, for he does not initially "get in David's face" and challenge him with his deeds. Instead, Nathan tells David a story about two neighbors, and that story will lead David to see his sins from God's point of view rather than from the world's.

## Keys to the Text

Read 2 Samuel 12:1–25, noting the key words and phrases indicated below.

NATHAN CONFRONTS DAVID: *David has married Bathsheba,*
*they have a new child, and it seems he has gotten away with*
*murder. But then God has His say in the matter.*

12:1. THEN THE LORD SENT NATHAN: It had probably been about a year since David's adultery with Bathsheba, and we can assume their child was at least a few months old at this time.

HE CAME TO HIM: Just as Joab had sent a messenger to David, so God would send His messenger to David—though it would not bring the same relief Joab's message had. Nathan would confront David not with a challenge but with a parable.

THERE WERE TWO MEN: It is interesting to note the differences between the men in Nathan's parable, who represented David and Uriah. One was rich and the other poor, which suggests Uriah was not a man of means. One had many flocks and herds and the other only one lamb, which shows Uriah was faithfully married only to Bathsheba. The rich man used his herds and flocks for food and income, while the poor man kept his lamb as a pet, which suggests the devoted love Uriah had for his wife.

3. LAY IN HIS BOSOM: If Nathan's parable represented an accurate picture of Uriah's household, then David's sin had destroyed a godly family.

4. A TRAVELER CAME TO THE RICH MAN: This is an illuminating metaphor of temptation, the lusts and desires of man's heart, which come and go without bidding. David had not intended to look for another man's wife; the temptation had come on him suddenly and unexpectedly.

REFUSED TO TAKE FROM HIS OWN FLOCK: David could easily have found comfort with one of his many wives, but that is not the nature of lust. Lust demands that which is forbidden or unattainable and makes what is good and proper seem detestable. The rich man in the proverb was wicked because he refused to sacrifice one of his many lambs and insisted on taking the poor man's cherished pet. This was exactly what David had done.

PREPARED IT FOR THE MAN WHO HAD COME TO HIM: David had sacrificed Bathsheba, Uriah, and others on the altar of his own lust, just as the rich man in the parable had sacrificed the poor man's lamb to satisfy the traveling salesman.

*THE KING PASSES JUDGMENT: David is outraged by Nathan's story and passes a harsh sentence on the rich man—thereby condemning himself to death.*

5. DAVID'S ANGER WAS GREATLY AROUSED: David took Nathan's story literally and believed someone in his kingdom had committed this grievous sin. Of course, someone had, but that someone was the king himself. David's anger also demonstrated he had finally seen his sin from God's perspective, and his righteous indignation was stirred. But he could not become indignant against his own sin until he saw it from God's viewpoint.

SHALL SURELY DIE: The law did not require the death penalty for stealing an ox or lamb, but merely restitution (see Exodus 22:1). In passing this harsh verdict, David was unwittingly condemning himself to death, which *was* the correct judgment for both murder and adultery (see Leviticus 20:10; 24:17).

6. HE SHALL RESTORE FOURFOLD FOR THE LAMB: According to the Law, this was the proper judgment for the crime of stealing a lamb. There is a certain dark and ironic humor in David condemning a man to death *and* restitution. David's judgment, which he pronounced in a cavalier fashion on a hypothetical stranger, would come on his own head.

BECAUSE HE HAD NO PITY: David had shown no pity to his faithful warrior Uriah. Even after committing adultery, he might have been moved by remorse for destroying another man's marriage. David's sin was actually greater than that of the rich man in the parable, for that man merely stole the poor man's lamb but didn't murder the poor man himself.

*THE LORD SPEAKS: Nathan now confronts David openly with his sin and pronounces the Lord's judgment, which is far less harsh than David's rash sentence.*

8. YOUR MASTER'S WIVES: God, in His providence, had given David everything that had belonged to King Saul. There is no evidence that David ever married any of Saul's wives, though at the time the harem of eastern kings passed to their successors.

I ALSO WOULD HAVE GIVEN YOU MUCH MORE: The Lord had blessed David beyond all measure, promising to establish his throne forever, and would willingly have given David even more if he had asked. God wants His children to ask Him to meet their needs rather than reach out for themselves and take what does not belong to them.

9. DESPISED THE COMMANDMENT OF THE LORD: To despise the word of the Lord was to break His commands and incur punishment (see Numbers 15:31). Disobeying God's commands demonstrates contempt for His Word and contempt for Christ, the Incarnate Word.

10. THE SWORD SHALL NEVER DEPART FROM YOUR HOUSE: David's tragic punishment would be a lingering one. As David had betrayed the sanctity of Uriah's marriage, so his son would betray his father's marriage bed. As David had brought the sword on an innocent man, so his sons would bring the sword on one another.

12. YOU DID IT SECRETLY: God promises those things we do in secret will be brought into the light of day for all to see. Jesus said, "For there is nothing hidden which will not be revealed, nor has anything been kept secret but that it should come to light" (Mark 4:22).

*DAVID REPENTS: Here we see one reason why David is called "a man after God's own heart." When he is confronted with his sin, he confesses immediately.*

13. I HAVE SINNED AGAINST THE LORD: David had sinned greatly, yet when confronted he did not try to justify his actions or blame his sin on

someone else. Instead, he confessed openly that he was guilty as charged. Notice also that David knew he had sinned against the *Lord*, not merely against Bathsheba, Uriah, and his soldiers.

THE LORD ALSO HAS PUT AWAY YOUR SIN: This is the glorious message of the gospel: God forgives even the most wicked sinners if they will confess and repent.

YOU SHALL NOT DIE: The Law demanded that murderers and adulterers be put to death, and David was guilty of both crimes. Yet God forgave David and set him free from that penalty, just as the sacrifice of Christ sets free those who accept His gift of salvation. Paul notes that "all have sinned and fall short of the glory of God" (Romans 3:23) and are therefore subject to death. Christ Himself paid the penalty for all who would receive Him, which satisfied God's justice while also offering grace to the guilty.

14. BECAUSE BY THIS DEED: The Lord's mercy applied to David's eternal relationship with God but did not exempt him from suffering the temporal consequences of his sin.

YOU HAVE GIVEN GREAT OCCASION TO THE ENEMIES OF THE LORD: David had displayed a contempt for God's Word, and the Lord Himself, because of his sin. Similarly, his sin would encourage the enemies of God to demonstrate contempt for the things of the Lord. Sin affects more than just those who are involved in it.

THE CHILD ALSO WHO IS BORN TO YOU SHALL SURELY DIE: Yet one more innocent life would be forfeited due to David's sin.

*JUDGMENT AND GRACE: The little child dies as God foretold, but God's grace follows His judgment. David and Bathsheba have another son, Solomon, who will become king.*

18. THE SERVANTS OF DAVID WERE AFRAID TO TELL HIM: The servants misunderstood David's weeping and fasting over the sick child. They assumed he was grieving, when in fact he was interceding for the child's life. When the child finally died, David knew the Lord's answer to his prayers had been no—and he had no further occasion to make that intercession.

20. HE WENT INTO THE HOUSE OF THE LORD AND WORSHIPED: Some might have become angry with God for taking the life of the child, but David recognized God had been both just and merciful. His response, even in the

midst of great sorrow, was to worship God. In this he again demonstrated what it means to be a man after God's own heart.

23. I SHALL GO TO HIM: David demonstrated great faith in God's promises, believing he would one day meet his son in eternity. It is clear David fully expected to see his baby again after his own death. Here is the confidence there is a future reunion after death.

24–25. SOLOMON . . . JEDIDIAH: David called his son "Solomon," which means either "[God is] peace" or "His replacement." Both were true of this child. Nathan called him "Jedidiah," which means "beloved of the Lord," and he was loved in the sense of being chosen by the Lord to be David's successor. God's immense grace had brought great blessing even out of gross sin.

## GOING DEEPER

David wrote Psalm 51 after Nathan confronted him with the sins he had committed. Read this psalm and note the key words and phrases below.

> A CRY FOR MERCY: *David's response after God brings his sin to light is to throw himself at the feet of the Lord and cry out for mercy.*

51:1. HAVE MERCY UPON ME: David confessed that he was guilty as charged and offered no excuses. He recognized he was entirely deserving of the Lord's anger.

ACCORDING TO YOUR LOVINGKINDNESS: David acknowledged that any mercy God showed to him would flow naturally out of the Lord's own kindness and generosity. Note that David was not asking for God to be kind; he understood that God *is* kind and loving. David's pleas for forgiveness were seasoned with the anticipation that his loving God would grant it.

BLOT OUT MY TRANSGRESSIONS: This image is of a written record of David's deeds that God completely expunged, erasing the sin so completely it was as if it had never happened.

2. WASH ME THOROUGHLY: David recognized his sins defiled him, making him filthy and unfit to approach God's presence. He knew cleansing could only come from the hand of God. Yet again, we get the sense of expectation that God will do it.

*CONFESSING HIS SINS: David does not try to explain away his guilt but confesses openly that he has sinned against the Lord.*

4. AGAINST YOU, YOU ONLY, HAVE I SINNED: David understood all sin is ultimately committed against God. He had pretended for many months the Lord didn't see his sin, but in his repentance he also came to acknowledge nothing is hidden from God.

5. IN SIN MY MOTHER CONCEIVED ME: David recognized he was a sinner from birth and that sin was part of his basic human nature. Everyone who has ever lived has sinned, because everyone is descended from Adam—everyone, that is, except Jesus. The apostle Paul confirmed this when he wrote, "For all have sinned and fall short of the glory of God" (Romans 3:23).

6. YOU DESIRE TRUTH IN THE INWARD PARTS: That is, in the inner man, the true nature of a person's character—that which is hidden from others but visible to God. "Truth in the inward parts" can only be produced by staying in God's Word. His truth searches a man's inmost being, cutting through all pretense and self-deception and bringing light and life (see Hebrews 4:12).

7. PURGE ME WITH HYSSOP: Hyssop was an aromatic plant used by priests to sprinkle blood or water on a person during ceremonial cleansing (see Leviticus 14:6). David was yearning for a complete cleansing from the defilement of his sin.

*A PRAYER FOR RESTORATION: David's concern is not that he will suffer punishment but that he is out of fellowship with God. His desire is to be restored.*

8. MAKE ME HEAR JOY AND GLADNESS: Here is another description of the deadening effect sin has on a person's spirit. All joy goes out of life, and things that once brought pleasure or satisfaction no longer do so. David's guilt was causing him extreme anguish, even to the point of physical symptoms (see also Psalm 32:3–4).

9. HIDE YOUR FACE FROM MY SINS: David wanted his sin to be so utterly eradicated that God would never look on it again. The opposite of this is when God turns His face away from the unrepentant sinner who refuses His offer of forgiveness. The Lord is always working to bring sinners to repentance,

and He will never turn His face away from the one who confesses sin. But the day will come when He will turn His back forever on those who have rejected Him.

10. **CREATE IN ME A CLEAN HEART:** The word translated *create* is the same word used in Genesis 1:1, "In the beginning God created the heavens and the earth." David recognized a pure heart was something only God could create. A pure heart does not naturally evolve in any man or woman, and humanity is powerless to create it.

11. **DO NOT CAST ME AWAY FROM YOUR PRESENCE:** The Lord gave Israel's leaders His Spirit, which empowered them to deliver His people from their enemies. When those kings or judges rejected God's leadership, He took His Spirit away from them. However, Christians will never experience the removal of the Holy Spirit, because they are permanently sealed in Christ.

13. **I WILL TEACH TRANSGRESSORS YOUR WAYS:** The glorious news of God's forgiveness brought joy and restoration to David, and it was only natural that he wanted to share it with others.

17. **THE SACRIFICES OF GOD ARE A BROKEN SPIRIT:** God did accept people's sacrifices in the Old Testament, but only when those sacrifices were accompanied by genuine repentance. God delights in the restored sinner rather than in the sacrificial offering. It is the *result* of the sacrifice—the restored relationship with His people—that brings God pleasure.

## UNLEASHING THE TEXT

1) Why did Nathan have to confront David about his sin? What prevented David from repenting sooner?

_____

_____

_____

_____

_____

2) How did Nathan's parable expose the true nature of David's sins? What elements in the parable related directly to those sins?

_____

_____

_____

3) Why did God say David had despised Him? In what ways do we despise God when we sin?

_____

_____

_____

4) Why did David go to the temple and worship God after his child died? What does this reveal about David's character?

_____

_____

_____

## EXPLORING THE MEANING

**God's people must view sin from God's perspective.** When David committed adultery, he viewed his actions from a human perspective. His major concern was to prevent other people from knowing what he had done, which led him to attempt a cover-up. As we have seen already, however, his cover-up led to more sin and further attempts to conceal it.

If David had viewed his sin of adultery from God's point of view, he would have been quick to confess and repent. Humans are concerned with what other people will think, but God is interested in how our sin damages our relationship with Him. David was worried about his reputation as king, while God was thinking of his eternal fellowship.

Today, the world tells us the most important priority is appearances. The world tells us to place value on outward show and claims there are no eternal consequences for our actions. God, however, is focused on eternity. He wants His people to see every sin as something that puts distance between them and Him.

**Sin brings temporal consequences that sometimes cannot be avoided.** When David confessed his sin and repented, the Lord showed him mercy and grace. The Law demanded that he should be put to death for both adultery and murder, but God commuted that sentence—and went even further by blessing him with Solomon. Nevertheless, the temporal results of David's sins were not removed. His family, and the nation, would suffer greatly for his transgressions.

God shows His infinite mercy to us when we repent. He provides us with forgiveness and eternal life—and much more. Yet there are times when our sinful behaviors will produce bad fruit that does not go away. We may retain scars or weaknesses that affect our lives and the lives of those we love. These results of former sins may remain with us for years or even a lifetime. This principle applies to Christians and non-Christians alike.

Sin can seem alluring during times of temptation, but the end result is always the same: *death*. As we learn to see from God's perspective, we will also see that in the end sin never pays. It is always best to live according to God's Word, for in this way we avoid the deadly scars and consequences that result otherwise.

**The man after God's own heart is quick to repent.** One can hardly say that David repented quickly after his sin of adultery, since it was probably a year or so later when Nathan confronted him. If he had confessed his adultery immediately, he would have avoided adding the sin of murder to his guilt. If he had repented immediately of his lust when gazing at Bathsheba, he would have avoided the adultery altogether.

Nevertheless, David did repent and confess immediately when he was brought face-to-face with his sin as God viewed it. In doing so, he demonstrated that he was a man after God's own heart. He recognized he had sinned against *the Lord*, not merely against his fellow man, and he understood that his sin had separated him from God's fellowship.

The goal for God's people should be to avoid sin altogether, but when we do sin, we should be quick to confess and repent. We cannot hope to hide our sins from God, so cover-ups are of no avail. When we delay confession, we only deprive ourselves of full fellowship with the Father and cheat ourselves out of His blessings.

## REFLECTING ON THE TEXT

5) Why did Nathan use a parable to confront David? Why not a direct accusation? What does this teach us about the nature of confession?

_____

_____

_____

6) Why did David condemn to death the rich man in Nathan's parable? What did this reveal about David's attitude toward his own guilt?

_____

_____

_____

7) Why did God not condemn David to die, even though the Law demanded the death penalty for both murder and adultery? What does this reveal about God's nature?

_____

_____

_____

8) Why did God not remove the judgment against David's family? What does this reveal about the nature of sin?

_____

_____

_____

## Personal Response

9) Are there any sins in your life of which you have not repented? What is preventing you from confessing them to the Lord right now?

_____

_____

_____

10) How does a person gain God's perspective concerning sin and holiness? What are you doing at present to gain that perspective?

_____

_____

_____

# 7

# TROUBLE IN DAVID'S HOUSE

*2 Samuel 13:1–39*

## DRAWING NEAR

What are some ways your parents showed you discipline when you were growing up? How can you look back now and appreciate their guidance in your life?

_____

_____

_____

## THE CONTEXT

In the previous study, we learned that after David's sin with Bathsheba and his attempted cover-up, the prophet Nathan confronted the king and brought a prophecy from the Lord that the sword would never depart from his household. It did not take long for this prophecy from God to begin to unfold. The events that followed would be tragic and heartbreaking.

David's household was ripe for such conflict, as he had numerous wives and concubines who had borne him many sons. That situation fostered jealousies and strife, especially as David's sons began vying for their father's throne. David's firstborn son was Amnon, whose mother was Ahinoam. By rights, Amnon was the natural successor to David's throne, but Absalom had other ideas. Absalom was born to Maacah, herself the daughter of a king, and he evidently felt himself better qualified to take his father's place.

But another problem also arose within David's mixed family: his eldest son developed an unhealthy desire for his half sister, Tamar. This dangerous situation was made all the more volatile because Amnon, the heir apparent, was lusting after the *full* sister of his rival Absalom. When Amnon acted on these unhealthy desires and ended up raping Tamar, he gave Absalom an excuse to murder him—and the seeds of revolution were sown.

## KEYS TO THE TEXT

Read 2 Samuel 13:1–39, noting the key words and phrases indicated below.

*LOVESICK: David has many wives and many children—which is a recipe for disaster. One of his sons begins to lust after his half sister.*

13:1. AFTER THIS: That is, sometime after David was confronted by Nathan concerning his adultery and murder. The author was letting us know that there was a connection between David's sin and what occurred in this chapter. The fulfillment of the Lord's prophecy that Nathan had declared in 2 Samuel 12:10 was beginning to unfold.

ABSALOM THE SON OF DAVID: David's third son, born to him through Maacah, his fourth wife. Maacah's father was Talmai, the King of Geshur, a land located to the east of the Sea of Galilee (see 2 Samuel 3:3). The territory had been allotted to the tribe of Manasseh, but they could not expel its inhabitants (see Joshua 13:13). David had many wives, and it will be important to understand the interrelationship between his children in this study as the rivalries and resentments become apparent.

WHOSE NAME WAS TAMAR: Her name means "palm tree." Her mother was also Maacah, which made her the full sister of Absalom.

AMNON THE SON OF DAVID: Amnon was David's son by Ahinoam, his second wife. Thus Amnon was a half brother to both Tamar and Absalom. He was also David's firstborn, which might have added some tension in his relationship with Absalom, the third-born son. By birthright Amnon was the heir to David's throne, while Absalom would receive little by way of inheritance. It is interesting to note there is no mention in this account of David's second son, Chileab (see 2 Samuel 3:3), which suggests he was no longer alive at this point.

LOVED HER: Amnon's love turned out to be merely lust, as this story will reveal.

2. HE BECAME SICK: The picture of the lovesick young man—pining away in unrequited longing for the woman of his dreams—is popular in modern art. But this chapter will demonstrate that such sentiments may only be a thin disguise for lust. Amnon was obsessed with his desire for his half sister to the point that he could think of nothing else. He was so distressed, in fact, that he could not even undertake his normal daily duties.

SHE WAS A VIRGIN: A woman's virginity in David's time was protected and cherished at all costs. Unmarried daughters were kept apart from men and were not even permitted to be in a man's company without family members present. Amnon, however, would have been in contact with Tamar because of their family relationship.

IT WAS IMPROPER FOR AMNON TO DO ANYTHING TO HER: It would have been inappropriate for a young man to have any intimacy with a woman to whom he was not married. However, the impropriety in this instance was even worse than that because the law forbade a man to marry his sister—even a half sister (see Leviticus 18:11).

*A CRAFTY COUNSELOR: David's nephew Jonadab is a cunning man, and he shares the subtle craftiness of the devil. His advice leads to disaster for David's household.*

3. JONADAB: This was the son of David's brother Shammah (see 1 Samuel 16:9) or Shimea (see 1 Chronicles 2:13), which made him Amnon's cousin.

A VERY CRAFTY MAN: Craftiness, or cunning, is not considered a virtue in Scripture. The serpent in Eden "was more cunning than any beast of the field which the Lord God had made" (Genesis 3:1), and his lies deceived Eve into eating the forbidden fruit. In a similar manner, the cunning of Jonadab would lead Amnon into acting on his lusts.

4. THE KING'S SON: On one hand, Jonadab was merely pointing out the obvious—that the son of the king should have everything he needed to keep him content. However, on a more subtle level he was flattering Amnon by suggesting that, as the heir apparent to his father's throne, he had a right to reach

out and take whatever he desired. Compare Satan's temptation of Eve when he challenged her by saying, "Has God indeed said, 'You shall not eat of every tree of the garden?'" (Genesis 3:1).

**5. PRETEND TO BE ILL:** Jonadab's counsel was wicked from the outset, as he suggested that Amnon deceive his father. A crafty person is deceitful and manipulative and uses the very same tools the devil used to deceive Eve.

**6. THAT I MAY EAT FROM HER HAND:** It was childish behavior to suggest that a grown man could not eat any food unless it was prepared in his sight by a specific person. The fact that David acquiesced suggests the king was excessively indulgent with his sons, as we will see more fully in David's dealings with Absalom.

**10. BRING THE FOOD INTO THE BEDROOM:** Amnon's sin was even more despicable when we see how he betrayed his sister's trust. Tamar unhesitatingly complied with his request because his wicked intentions never entered her mind. She was the one character in this tragic tale who showed no guile, and it was she who suffered the most.

*TAMAR PLEADS FOR RIGHTEOUSNESS: Tamar demonstrates that she has a heart for God and wants to do what is right. But her brother refuses to listen.*

**12. NO SUCH THING SHOULD BE DONE IN ISRAEL:** Tamar made every attempt to escape the clutches of lustful Amnon, giving him three clear reasons why he should not force himself on her. The first reason, and the most significant one, was that such an act was forbidden by God's law and as such should not be committed by any of God's people. Tamar knew that such action could bring disharmony and bloodshed to the family, as it ultimately did.

**13. WHERE COULD I TAKE MY SHAME:** Tamar's second argument against Amnon's behavior was to point out that he would bring shame on her if he continued. Even though she was fighting for her innocence, she would probably be unable to find a man who wanted to marry her once she had lost her virginity. She would be disgraced in David's court.

**YOU WOULD BE LIKE ONE OF THE FOOLS IN ISRAEL:** Tamar's third argument was to point out that Amnon would also bring disgrace on himself if he continued. The people would recognize that he cared more about his own passions than about obeying God's commands, which might also jeopardize his claims to his father's throne in the future. Tamar was trying to make her brother see that he was sinning against God, against her, and against himself.

HE WILL NOT WITHHOLD ME FROM YOU: As already stated, such a marriage was forbidden by God's law, so it was unlikely that David would actually have sanctioned it. Yet Tamar was in a desperate situation and was urging her brother to restrain his passions.

14. HE FORCED HER: A euphemism for "raped."

15. AMNON HATED HER EXCEEDINGLY: This is generally the sad result of indulged lusts. Once the desire is sated, the former attraction turns to revulsion. Amnon's hatred was probably based on a degree of self-loathing as he saw the immense wickedness he had committed. This would be yet another bad way for him to deal with his passions. Rather than hating his sister, whom he had wronged, he should have hated his own sin and sought forgiveness from God and from his family. In this, we find a strong contrast to David's response when he was confronted with his sin: David repented, but Amnon blamed others.

16. THIS EVIL OF SENDING ME AWAY: Tamar feared it would appear to others as though she had willingly cooperated with her brother's sin, or even that she had initiated it.

17. BOLT THE DOOR BEHIND HER: Amnon disgraced his sister yet further when he called in a servant and had her thrown out, effectively signaling to the household that she had seduced him. Bolting the door behind her gave the appearance that Amnon feared she might try to come back and lead him into more sin.

*TAMAR'S SHAME: Tamar flees to her brother Absalom, who gives her some very bad advice for coping with the situation. Meanwhile, he begins to quietly plot his revenge.*

18. ROBE OF MANY COLORS: This was a garment that identified the wearer's special position. For Tamar, the robe identified her as a virgin daughter of the king. The tearing of this robe symbolized her loss of this special position.

19. TAMAR PUT ASHES ON HER HEAD: Tamar's response to this sin contrasts dramatically with that of Amnon. The ashes on her head, the torn robe, and the loud lamenting were a public declaration of grief, shame, and loss. Amnon hoped to hide his sin, as David had done, while Tamar realized that sin cannot remain hidden.

20. DO NOT TAKE THIS THING TO HEART: Absalom's counsel was as bad as that of Jonadab, for he told his sister not to pay undue attention or worry about the consequences of the rape. He was saying, in effect, that sin is nothing to worry about—and his counsel is still given by the world today. In truth, however, Absalom had his own plans for revenge. He probably saw this event as an excuse to remove his brother Amnon from the succession to the throne.

TAMAR REMAINED DESOLATE: Tamar remained unmarried and childless under the protection of Absalom, her full brother. At the time, the children of polygamist unions lived by themselves in different family units.

21. HE WAS VERY ANGRY: David's wrath was justified, and he should have addressed the sin with quick action. But there is no record he did anything about it, and it is quite possible he felt it would have been hypocritical of him to punish Amnon after he had committed similar sins himself. Whatever his motivation, David did not fulfill his obligations either as king or as Tamar's father. This lack of justice would come back to haunt David in a future day.

22. ABSALOM HATED AMNON: Just as Amnon hated Tamar, so Absalom loathed his half-brother Amnon.

*ABSALOM GETS REVENGE: David has failed to address the sin of Amnon, so Absalom plots evil and takes matters into his own hands. Absalom eventually murders his half brother.*

23. ABSALOM HAD SHEEPSHEARERS IN BAAL HAZOR: Absalom put on this sheep-shearing feast in the Benjamite village of Hazor, located about twelve miles northeast of Jerusalem. He invited all his brothers, his half brothers, his father (the king), and the king's royal court to attend.

25. NO, MY SON, LET US NOT ALL GO NOW: David declined the offer, but he encouraged Absalom to hold the feast for "the king's sons" as a means of promoting unity and harmony. When David refused the invitation, Absalom requested that Amnon go as his representative. David had reservations about Absalom's intent, but he still allowed all his sons to go.

28. ABSALOM HAD COMMANDED HIS SERVANTS: It is interesting that both Absalom and Amnon used their servants to do their dirty work. In many ways they were mimicking the actions of their father, who had his general, Joab, arrange the murder of Uriah in battle.

KILL HIM: Amnon had committed the sin of sexual immorality like his father, and now Absalom—also like his father—would commit the sin of murder.

In this Absalom may have been motivated by the hopes of securing the throne for himself, as Amnon's death would make him the heir apparent. The Law did prescribe the death penalty for Amnon's crime (see Leviticus 18), but it was not Absalom's place to execute that judgment.

29. HIS MULE: The royal family in David's time rode mules. Later kings of his lineage would do the same (see 1 Kings 1:33, 38, 44).

30. ALL THE KING'S SONS: When the news of what had transpired at Absalom's sheep-shearing feast reached David, it contained the exaggerated report that all of his sons had been killed. This plunged David and his household into grief until Jonadab corrected it. He said to the king, "Let not my lord suppose they have killed all the young men, the king's sons, for only Amnon is dead. For by the command of Absalom this has been determined from the day that he forced his sister Tamar" (2 Samuel 13:32–33).

33. LET NOT MY LORD THE KING TAKE THE THING TO HIS HEART: Here we find Jonadab offering the same wicked counsel to David as Absalom had given earlier. The wisdom of the world tells us to gloss over sin, but God's Word teaches clearly that sin brings consequences.

37. ABSALOM FLED: The law regarding premeditated murder, as most would view Absalom's act, gave him no hope of returning (see Numbers 35:21). The cities of refuge would afford him no sanctuary, so he left his father's kingdom to live in Geshur, located east of the Sea of Galilee. There he would be under the protection of the king who was the grandfather of both Tamar and Absalom. David's household was falling apart, just as God had predicted.

39. LONGED TO GO: David gradually accepted the fact of Amnon's death and desired to see Absalom again, but he took no action to bring him back.


## UNLEASHING THE TEXT

1) Why was Amnon so consumed with desire for Tamar? What was the nature of his "love" for her?

_____

_____

_____

2) What reasons did Tamar give to her brother for avoiding sin? How do these concepts apply to sin in general?

_____

_____

_____

3) Why did Amnon come to despise Tamar? What does this reveal about his desires? What does it reveal about sin in general?

_____

_____

_____

4) What was ungodly in Jonadab's counsel to Amnon? What was ungodly in his counsel to David? Why did each man accept his counsel rather than reject it?

_____

_____

_____

## EXPLORING THE MEANING

***God's people must restrain their fleshly desires.*** In the story told in 2 Samuel 11, we saw how David arose from a nap and inadvertently saw a woman bathing. If he had turned away, he would not have become consumed with desire for her. But instead, he permitted his desires to have their way, and he ended up committing adultery. His son Amnon later followed his example by not reining in his lust for Tamar, and that lust bore horrible fruit.

Temptation comes to all people. As long as we live in fleshly bodies, we will experience physical desires. It is important to recognize that the desire itself is not sin—the sin comes when we yield to desires that are contrary to God's Word. For instance, it is not a sin to become hungry, but it can be a sin when we yield to the temptation of gluttony.

God wants His children to be characterized by self-control. The world teaches that we should gratify our every desire and claims that it is not healthy for us to restrain our natural impulses. But God's Word warns us that the cravings of the flesh lead to death, while righteousness evidenced by self-control leads to life. "As righteousness leads to life, so he who pursues evil pursues it to his own death" (Proverbs 11:19).

**Revenge belongs to God.** Amnon's sin was grievous, and it needed to be addressed. This was David's job as king, and he should not have ignored the sin even though his own son had committed it. Nevertheless, this did not justify Absalom's taking the matter into his own hands. When Absalom killed Amnon, he did not exact justice but carried out his own revenge. By doing so, he was merely committing another gross sin before God, and not carrying out God's design.

It is a natural human response to want justice, and this in itself is not wrong. Yet God's people do well to remember that we do not receive what we deserve from God—we receive grace, not condemnation. When someone harms us in some way, our flesh wants to get even and demands that justice be served. But this is another facet of restraining our fleshly desires and choosing instead to forgive and leave the matter in God's hands.

People after God's own heart will even go beyond refraining from taking revenge by actually doing good to those who have harmed them. Jesus said, "Love your enemies, bless those who curse you, do good to those who hate you, and pray for those who spitefully use you and persecute you, that you may be sons of your Father in heaven" (Matthew 5:44–45). This is exactly what Christ did for us, pouring out blessings on us when all we deserved was death.

**Beware of ungodly counsel.** Jonadab saw that Amnon was pining away after a woman, so he offered advice on how to gratify his carnal cravings. And, like most false counselors, he seemed to be well versed in the intrigues of everyone around him, appearing at the most opportune times to give his advice, as he did when David was grieving.

Jonadab began his counsel to Amnon by suggesting that the young man deceive his father. He said, "Lie down on your bed and pretend to be ill. And when your father comes to see you, say to him, 'Please let my sister Tamar come and give me food, and prepare the food in my sight, that I may see it and eat it from her hand'" (2 Samuel 13:5). Amnon should have recognized that Jonadab's advice was ungodly and rejected it outright. Instead, he followed Jonadab's poisonous "wisdom," though he was not compelled to do so.

Today, the world bombards us with ungodly counsel that, like Jonadab's advice, often sounds wise and expedient. But God's people are called to weigh every teaching against the teachings of Scripture, and godly counsel never advises us to disobey God's commands. Had Amnon considered that fact, he may actually have succeeded his father on the throne.

## REFLECTING ON THE TEXT

5) What should Amnon have done about his desires for Tamar? What would have been a godly way of dealing with the situation?

_____

_____

_____

_____

6) How did the actions of Amnon and Absalom mirror David's life? How did they differ?

_____

_____

_____

7) Why did David not address the sin of Amnon? Why did he not address Absalom's sin? How might things have ended if he had punished Amnon in the first place?

_____

_____

_____

8) What role did Jonadab play in these two tragedies? How much responsibility did he bear for the sins committed? How much responsibility did Amnon and Absalom bear?

_____

_____

_____

## PERSONAL RESPONSE

9) When have you received ungodly counsel? How can you tell when someone is giving you godly advice?

_____

_____

_____

10) Is there an area of fleshly desire that is controlling your life at present? What must you do to restrain those desires?

_____

_____

_____

# 8

# Absalom's Rebellion

*2 Samuel 15:1–37*

## Drawing Near

In what ways is ambition a good characteristic to have? It what ways can it be a negative influence over a person's life?

_____

_____

_____

## The Context

After Absalom murdered his brother Amnon, he fled Jerusalem and went to live with his grandfather, the king of Geshur. He lived there for three years, while David mourned for him and yearned to see him again. Joab, the commander of Israel's army, eventually intervened (using a tactic similar to Nathan's previous confrontation) and persuaded the king to send word to Absalom, permitting him to return to Jerusalem.

However, once Absalom returned, David refused to see him. Perhaps in this David was torn between his fatherly love and his guilt over the fact that he had not executed justice after the murder of Amnon. Whatever his motives,

Absalom was forced to content himself living in Jerusalem without access to his father. In this, however, he was anything but content.

So Absalom took matters into his own hands. He had his servants set fire to Joab's crops, which forced a confrontation between the two men. Joab finally went to David and interceded on Absalom's behalf, and David relented and restored his son to a full loving relationship. One might expect that Absalom would be content with this outcome. After all, what more could he desire once he had been restored to David's good graces?

As it turns out, there was much more that Absalom desired. He lusted for power and would not be satisfied until he had killed his father and taken the throne for himself. In this study, we will see yet another tragic element of the Lord's prophecy that the sword would never depart from David's house (see 2 Samuel 12:10).

## KEYS TO THE TEXT

Read 2 Samuel 15:1–37, noting the key words and phrases indicated below.

> PLAYING POLITICS: *Time passes, and David's son Absalom decides it is high time he was king. He soon sets about building a conspiracy against David.*

15:1. AFTER THIS IT HAPPENED: The events in this chapter took place after Joab had persuaded David to permit Absalom to return to Jerusalem (see 2 Samuel 14).

ABSALOM PROVIDED HIMSELF WITH CHARIOTS AND HORSES: Absalom began to take on the outward appearance of royalty, driving throughout the land in expensive chariots as men ran before him and announced his approach. In effect, Absalom was giving himself a parade whenever he ventured out in public. The Lord had previously warned the people of Israel through the prophet Samuel that kings would behave in this manner (see 1 Samuel 8:11).

2. ABSALOM WOULD RISE EARLY: The city gate was the site of public hearings on many civil matters that were usually resolved by the city's elders. Such hearings were conducted in the early morning hours, before the heat of the day. Absalom deliberately took up a conspicuous position at the city gates in order to set himself up as a sort of judge among the people.

ABSALOM WOULD CALL TO HIM: Absalom went beyond passively standing at the city gates and waiting for people to bring their complaints to him. He deliberately accosted people who were on their way to seek an audience with David.

3. YOUR CASE IS GOOD AND RIGHT: Absalom used flattery to gain the trust of those who had grievances. He did not concern himself with justice, and it appears he made no effort to look into the validity of anyone's claims. His desire was not for justice but for power.

THERE IS NO DEPUTY OF THE KING TO HEAR YOU: Absalom then took his plot to another level. He did not stop at offering a sort of drive-through justice but also told the people that David was too busy to look after his people's concerns. In this way, Absalom planted the early seeds of discontent and revolution in the people's minds.

4. OH, THAT I WERE MADE JUDGE IN THE LAND: Here we find an astute political ploy. Absalom first invented a grievance for the people to hold against David by suggesting that the king was too busy to provide them justice, and then he offered them the solution to that invented grievance. This ploy can still be observed in modern politics.

I WOULD GIVE HIM JUSTICE: In spite of Absalom's wicked intent, there was some truth in his claim of injustice within David's court. David had evidently been busy with other matters or with wars, and he was also aging, so many matters had been left unresolved. This had built a deep feeling of resentment among the people that Absalom used to his advantage. In this way, he won many of the people to himself, without them knowing his wicked ambition. The sad irony, of course, was that Absalom had benefited from this very lack of justice in the land by murdering his brother and getting away with it.

5. HE WOULD PUT OUT HIS HAND AND TAKE HIM AND KISS HIM: Absalom was essentially running for office, giving himself a parade, making public speeches, offering empty promises, shaking hands—stopping just short of kissing babies. A monarchy, however, is not an elected office. Absalom was deliberately stirring up rebellion against God's king.

*STEALING HEARTS: Absalom's tactics bear evil fruit, and he steals the nation's loyalty away from the rightful king.*

6. ABSALOM STOLE THE HEARTS OF THE MEN OF ISRAEL: A national hero will often be said to have won the hearts of the people through great deeds

of valor and patriotism. This was certainly true of David, who won the hearts of the Israelites through his acts of valor, such as the defeat of Goliath. This was a dire contrast to Absalom's theft of the people's loyalty.

7. AFTER FORTY YEARS: Other manuscripts translate this "four years." This is a better reading, as the number *forty* could refer neither to the age of Absalom, because he was born at Hebron after David had begun to rule (see 2 Samuel 3:2–5), nor the time of David's reign, because he ruled only forty years total (see 5:4–5). Absalom was probably around thirty years old at this time, and this four-year period began either with his return from Geshur or his reconciliation with David (see 4:23, 33). Given this evidence, it is likely this event occurred during the final decade of David's rule.

GO TO HEBRON: Absalom was born in Hebron, the place where David was first anointed king over Judah (see 2 Samuel 2:4). Its location, about twenty miles south of Jerusalem, afforded him enough distance from the king to keep his preparations hidden. Absalom said he had made a vow while in Geshur that if he was restored to Jerusalem, he would offer a sacrifice of thanksgiving in Hebron, where sacrifices were often made before the temple was built. David, who always encouraged such religious devotion, gave his consent.

11. THEY WENT ALONG INNOCENTLY: Absalom had previously lured his brothers to a sheep-shearing celebration in order to murder Amnon. He had then stolen the hearts of the Israelites by playing on their implicit trust in his integrity when he sat at the city gate. In this instance, he probably selected some of the most influential men in Jerusalem and led them on a sinister errand to Hebron, while they believed it to be a legitimate trip to fulfill a vow to the Lord. Manipulation was characteristic of Absalom's life, but he would not have been able to do this against his father if David had not been so lax in rebuking him (see 1 Kings 1:6).

12. AHITHOPHEL THE GILONITE: Ahithophel was Bathsheba's grandfather and one of David's trusted counselors. His advice was highly prized, but his decision to side with Absalom—possibly to take revenge on David for his adultery and murder—was not wise and ultimately led him to a tragic end. "Do not say, 'I will do him just as he has done to me; I will render to the man according to his work'" (Proverbs 24:29).

FROM GILOH: A town in the hill country of Judah, probably located a few miles south of Hebron (see Joshua 15:48, 51).

*DAVID'S ESCAPE: David is too late in recognizing the conspiracy against him, for the people's hearts are now with Absalom. He quickly makes his escape and flees for his life.*

**13. THE HEARTS OF THE MEN OF ISRAEL ARE WITH ABSALOM:** This is a sad statement of the fickleness of the human heart. David had done much good for the nation of Israel, and the Lord had blessed His people through his reign. Yet the Israelites turned against him in an instant when they were seduced by Absalom's vain flattery and deception.

**14. ARISE, AND LET US FLEE:** David wanted to avoid a bloodbath in the city of Jerusalem, whose very name was connected with the Hebrew word *shalom* (meaning "peace"), and also likely believed that he could find great support in the country. So he left the city with all his household and his personal guards.

**16. THE KING LEFT TEN WOMEN:** David would have assumed these women would be safe, since Absalom's concern was to kill his father, not his father's concubines. But in leaving them behind, David unwittingly set the stage for the fulfillment of the Lord's prophecies, as Absalom used them to disgrace David (2 Samuel 16:20–23).

**18. ALL THE CHERETHITES, ALL THE PELETHITES, AND ALL THE GITTITES:** These were foreign mercenary soldiers of King David. The Cherethites appear to have come from Crete, and the Gittites were Philistine soldiers from Gath.

**19. ITTAI THE GITTITE:** The commander of the Gittites, who had only recently joined David. In spite of David's words that he should return to Jerusalem, Ittai displayed his loyalty by choosing to go into exile with him. David would later appoint Ittai commander of one-third of the army as a way of expressing his appreciation for this loyalty.

**23. CROSSED OVER THE BROOK KIDRON:** This familiar valley, running north to south along the eastern side of Jerusalem, separated the city from the Mount of Olives.

**24. THERE WAS ZADOK:** Zadok, whose name means "righteous," was a Levitical priest descended from Aaron through Eleazar (see 1 Chronicles 6:3–8, 50–53). Later, he became the only high priest during Solomon's reign, fulfilling God's promise in Numbers 25:10–13 to Phinehas and his descendants.

BEARING THE ARK: Zadok and Abiathar, another priest, brought the ark of the covenant to comfort David and assure him of God's blessing. However, David saw this as placing more confidence in the symbol than in God, so he instructed the priests to send it back. David knew that merely possessing the ark did not guarantee God's blessing.

28. PLAINS OF THE WILDERNESS: This was probably the region along the western bank of the Jordan River.

30. MOUNT OF OLIVES: This hill, to the east of the city of Jerusalem, was the location for David's contrition and remorse over his past sins and their results. This was the same location from which Jesus would later ascend into heaven (see Acts 1:9–12).

32. TOP OF THE MOUNTAIN: From this high vantage point, David could look toward the city and the temple to the west.

HUSHAI THE ARCHITE: Hushai was of the clan of the Archites who lived in Ephraim on the border with Manasseh (see Joshua 16:2). He served as an official counselor to David (see 1 Chronicles 27:33). David persuaded Hushai to return to Jerusalem and attach himself to Absalom as his counselor. Hushai's mission was to contradict the advice of Ahithophel and to communicate Absalom's plans back to David.

## GOING DEEPER

David wrote Psalm 3 and, likely, Psalm 63 after Absalom's rebellion forced him to flee Jerusalem. Read these psalms and note the key words and phrases below.

> DAVID'S TRUST IN THE LORD: *In spite of David's mounting troubles, he recognizes the Lord has not abandoned him. For David, God is his shield and his protection.*

3:1. THEY HAVE INCREASED WHO TROUBLE ME: David began on a low note in this psalm by recounting his miseries brought about by the rebellion of his son Absalom.

3. YOU, O LORD, ARE A SHIELD FOR ME: David painted a strong contrast in this verse between those who alleged there was no help for him and his own faith in God's promises. David's attitude and outlook embraced the

theology that Paul summarized in Romans 8:31: "What then shall we say to these things? If God is for us, who can be against us?"

5. I LAY DOWN AND SLEPT: David knew God for His sustaining protection, so he could relax in the most trying of circumstances.

7. ARISE, O LORD; SAVE ME, O MY GOD: This is David's battle cry for God to engage the enemy and defend his soldiers.

8. SALVATION BELONGS TO THE LORD: This is a broad-sweeping and all-inclusive deliverance, whether in the temporal or eternal realm.

DAVID'S JOY IN THE LORD: *Even in the midst of trials, David expresses his deep devotion and love for the Lord. It is yet another demonstration of how he was a man after God's own heart.*

63:1. EARLY WILL I SEEK YOU: David had in view here his eagerness to be with the Lord in every situation, more than a specific time of day.

MY SOUL THIRSTS FOR YOU: David longed for God's presence like a wanderer in a desert longed for water.

IN A DRY AND THIRSTY LAND: Although David was writing this psalm while hiding in the wilderness of Judea, he longed to be back worshiping God in Jerusalem.

3. BETTER THAN LIFE: For David, God's covenant love with him was more valuable than life itself. Paul would later express a similar attitude when he said, "None of these things move me; nor do I count my life dear to myself, so that I may finish my race with joy, and the ministry which I received from the Lord Jesus, to testify to the gospel of the grace of God" (Acts 20:24).

4. LIFT UP MY HANDS: An Old Testament posture of prayer in which the upheld hands of the worshiper pictured both the ascent of prayer and the person's readiness to receive every good gift that came from God (see James 1:17). It represented a posture of trust in God alone.

5. MARROW AND FATNESS: A metaphor by which David compared the spiritual and emotional satisfaction of God's divine presence with the satisfaction of rich banquet food.

8. MY SOUL FOLLOWS CLOSE BEHIND YOU: David clung to God in response to the Lord's repeated invitation to "hold fast" to Him (see Deuteronomy 4:4). This signified David's unfailing commitment to his Lord.

9. INTO THE LOWER PARTS OF THE EARTH: A reference to the realm of the dead.

10. A PORTION FOR JACKALS: Jackals were scavengers who feasted on unburied bodies.

11. WHO SWEARS BY HIM: The Mosaic covenant instructed God's people to follow this practice and express loyalty to the true God alone (see Deuteronomy 6:13).

## UNLEASHING THE TEXT

1) Why did Absalom rebel against his father? What motivated him? How should he have lived his life?

_____

_____

_____

2) How might things have been different if David had executed justice after the murder of Amnon? After the rape of Tamar?

_____

_____

_____

3) Why did the people follow Absalom so readily and turn their backs on David? What did they hope to gain?

_____

_____

_____

4) How do the psalms David wrote during this time show that he was still a man after God's own heart?

_____

_____

_____

_____

_____

## EXPLORING THE MEANING

***We are to humble ourselves, not to exalt ourselves.*** Absalom was a man with immense charisma who was renowned for his good looks and magnetic personality. Moreover, he had the best pedigree one could hope for, as his father was a king and his mother was the daughter of a king. He was also gifted politically and was able to persuade people to his point of view. In short, he had the potential to become a very able leader in Israel.

Yet the great irony of Absalom's life is that by trying to lift himself up, he ended up being cast down. His attitude was the opposite of his father's. David had consistently humbled himself before Saul, even when it put his life in danger. He understood an important principle of God's Word: when God's people humble themselves, God will lift them up.

The world teaches us that if we don't look out for ourselves, nobody else will. But God's Word teaches the opposite. Christians don't need to be always looking after their own interests, because we can depend on God to care for us. As James reminds us, "Humble yourselves in the sight of the Lord, and He will lift you up" (James 4:10).

***Rebellion against God's king is never ultimately successful.*** Absalom probably considered himself to be the heir of David's throne, though that was not God's plan for his life. Absalom was overcome with his desire for power, and that lust led him to take matters into his own hands. He failed to realize that Israel's king was God's chosen servant. If Absalom had understood that rebelling against David was as likely to succeed as rebelling against God, his life might have ended in less disgrace.

This was a lesson the Jewish leaders—and Judas—learned in the New Testament. The Jews were looking for their Messiah, but they rejected Jesus because, rather than empowering them, He called them to repentance. Jesus' own disciple Judas, instead of receiving and serving God's king, arranged to have Him killed, and the Jewish leaders were eager to assist. Under God's sovereignty, their very act of treason—the cross—established Jesus' authority and affirmed His kingship, while Judas died a gruesome death (see Matthew 27:1–5).

Absalom learned the same lesson. By rebelling and overthrowing God's king, he brought about a course of events that would ultimately end with his own death.

***Guard your heart against the world's seductions.*** One of the most tragic elements of these passages in 2 Samuel 15 is the ease with which God's people turned against His chosen king. However, this is not hard to understand from a human perspective, because Absalom was a charismatic leader who knew how to play politics skillfully. He played on people's discontentment and fears, promising them a solution he could not deliver.

The world has not changed since David's day. There are still many forces that play on our frustrations and desires, making promises that cannot be fulfilled. We find these vain promises in politics, in advertising, in entertainment, and even from some pulpits—promises of temporal wealth, fleshly gratification, personal fulfillment, and much more. The world appeals to our vanity, just as Absalom did when he paraded himself through Jerusalem, and it plays on our fears and dissatisfactions, just as Absalom did with those he met at the city gates.

Remember the words David wrote at the very time when his life and kingship were in gravest danger: "Many are they who rise up against me. Many are they who say of me, 'There is no help for him in God.' . . . But You, O LORD, are a shield for me, my glory and the One who lifts up my head" (Psalm 3:1–3). True satisfaction and fulfillment can only be found in God; what the world promises cannot compare with what He promises.

## Reflecting on the Text

5) What events led up to Absalom's revolution? What part did David's sin play in setting the stage?

_____

_____

_____

6) What tactics did Absalom use to gain power? How does the world use these same tactics today to lead people away from God?

_____

_____

_____

7) Why does God command His people to humble themselves? How is this contrary to the world's teachings? How did Jesus demonstrate humility?

_____

_____

_____

8) In practical terms, how does the world try to seduce people away from God today? How can a Christian guard against those seductions?

_____

_____

_____

## PERSONAL RESPONSE

9) Are you trusting the sovereignty of God in your present circumstances, or are you struggling to take control? What Scripture passages might encourage you in this area?

_____

_____

_____

10) In what circumstances are you most tempted to exalt yourself rather than humble yourself? What can you learn in this regard from the example of Christ?

_____

_____

# 9

# ABSALOM'S DEFEAT
*2 Samuel 18:1–19:15*

## DRAWING NEAR

What are some ways you have seen pride lead to a person's downfall? What does that tell us about the importance of not thinking too highly of ourselves?

_____

_____

_____

_____

## THE CONTEXT

As we saw in the previous study, Absalom was able to subtly win the people's hearts through his political tactics and charisma. Ultimately, so many of the Israelites came to his side that David was forced to flee from the city of Jerusalem. As David ascended the Mount of Olives, weeping as he went, he encountered his servant Hushai. David, knowing this man's skills, sent him back to Jerusalem to foil the counsel Absalom was receiving. He also instructed Hushai to relay Absalom's plans to him through two priests who had remained loyal to him.

This would prove to be an effective strategy, for Absalom was now receiving counsel from Ahithophel, the grandfather of Bathsheba, whose advice was considered so wise and sound it was "as if one had inquired at the oracle of God" (2 Samuel 16:23). One of Ahithophel's first counsels to Absalom was for him to take possession of his father's harem and, in this way, assert his right to the throne. A tent on the roof of the palace was set up so the public could witness this event, thus fulfilling the judgment announced by Nathan in 2 Samuel 12:11–12.

Ahithophel's second piece of advice was for Absalom to immediately pursue and kill David. This was politically sound, but the Lord took control of the situation through the counsel of Hushai, who advised Absalom in such a way as to give David time to prepare for battle. For Absalom, Hushai's plan seemed the best course because it called for an army larger than twelve thousand men (so Absalom would not lose) and for him to lead the army personally (which played on his vanity). Hushai was then able to send a message to David to warn him to escape.

When Ahithophel saw that his counsel to Absalom had not been followed, he saddled his donkey, traveled back to his home, and hanged himself. His reason for doing so was likely motivated by his knowledge that Absalom would be defeated and that David would hold him accountable for his disloyalty. In this, we see that God had determined for Absalom's revolt to be defeated and that He was controlling all the intrigues among the usurper's counselors.

In time, Absalom was able to gather his vast host and commence his attack against David. He chose Amasa, one of Joab's relations, to lead his army and marched into the land of Gilead. The two sides now squared off to fight a battle that would decide the throne of Israel.

## KEYS TO THE TEXT

Read 2 Samuel 18:1–19:15, noting the key words and phrases indicated below.

*DAVID'S PLEA: As David's forces prepare for battle against Absalom, the king issues a command to his generals to deal gently with his rebellious son.*

18:2. DAVID SENT OUT ONE THIRD OF THE PEOPLE: It was a customary military strategy of the day to divide the army in such a way as to form a three-pronged attack.

3. YOU SHALL NOT GO OUT: David wanted to lead his men personally into the battle. However, the people recognized that his death would mean sure defeat and that Absalom would be secure in the kingship. The people's words echo what Ahithophel had earlier pointed out to Absalom (see 1 Samuel 17:2–3). So David was persuaded to remain at Mahanaim.

5. DEAL GENTLY: David ordered his three commanders not to harm Absalom. The four uses of "the young man Absalom" (verses 5, 12, 29, 32) imply that David sentimentally viewed Absalom as a youthful rebel who could be forgiven.

6. THE WOODS OF EPHRAIM: This was a dense forest that existed east of the Jordan River and north of the Jabbok River in Gilead, where the battle was waged.

8. THE WOODS DEVOURED MORE: Amazingly, because of the density of the trees and the rugged nature of the terrain, the army's pursuit through the forest resulted in more deaths than the actual combat.

*THE DEATH OF ABSALOM: In spite of David's pleas, Joab recognizes the danger of leaving Absalom alive and takes the opportunity to kill him. In this way the Lord's prophecies come to pass.*

9. HIS HEAD CAUGHT IN THE TEREBINTH: Either Absalom's neck was caught in a fork formed by two branches growing out from a terebinth (a tree native to Israel) or his hair was caught in a tangle of thick branches. The terminology and context favor the latter view. Absalom took great pride in his long, thick hair and in his good looks (see 2 Samuel 14:25–26), and there is a certain irony that this would be the cause of his death.

HANGING BETWEEN HEAVEN AND EARTH: This poetic phrase describes the literal situation of Absalom as he was dangling by his hair, but it also suggests the perilous circumstances he had created for himself as he suddenly found himself without any allies—either on earth or in heaven. Even the very mule on which he was riding abandoned him to his fate.

10. A CERTAIN MAN SAW IT: One of David's soldiers, who refused to disobey the order of the king to treat Absalom "gently," saw the prince suspended from the tree and reported it to Joab.

11. TEN SHEKELS OF SILVER: Joab told the man he would have given him ten shekels of silver, which represents approximately four ounces, if he had

struck down Absalom. The man refused, saying he would not have killed Absalom for a thousand shekels, which represents approximately twenty-five pounds.

12. BEWARE LEST ANYONE TOUCH THE YOUNG MAN ABSALOM: David had clearly commanded his three generals (Joab, Abishai, and Ittai) to squelch the rebellion but not to harm his son. This unnamed soldier was wise to disobey his commander at this point, for he knew to take Absalom's life would go directly against the king's command. It is likely this soldier also realized that Joab would later allow him to take the blame.

14. HE TOOK THREE SPEARS IN HIS HAND: Joab ultimately took matters into his own hands and thrust three spears into Absalom's heart to kill him. After this, his armor bearers struck Absalom to make sure he was dead.

15. STRUCK AND KILLED HIM: By this act Joab disobeyed the king's clear command, but he brought about a quick conclusion to the civil war and prevented further unnecessary deaths—and also carried out the justice that David had failed to exact by putting Absalom to death. So it was that David's own son died by the sword in fulfillment of the Lord's prophecy that the "sword shall never depart" from David's house (2 Samuel 12:10). Absalom had brought on himself the judgment of death when he murdered his own brother, and he had brought further condemnation by trying to overthrow God's anointed king.

16. BLEW THE TRUMPET: In this way, Joab recalled his soldiers from the battle.

17. A VERY LARGE HEAP OF STONES: The soldiers buried Absalom in a deep pit and covered it over with stones, perhaps symbolizing stoning, which was the legal penalty for a rebel son. A heap of stones often showed that the person buried was a criminal or enemy.

18. SET UP A PILLAR FOR HIMSELF: Today, orthodox Jews spit on a monument in this area—perhaps on the same site—called Absalom's tomb. This is the sad summary of Absalom's life, a man who set himself above all others. Saul, another man who was motivated by self-interest, also set up a monument to himself (see 1 Samuel 15:12)—and look where it got him.

*DAVID MOURNS: When David receives the news that his son Absalom has been killed in battle, he is deeply grieved and weeps bitterly.*

18. IN THE KING'S VALLEY: Traditionally this refers to the Kidron Valley, located immediately east of the city of Jerusalem.

I HAVE NO SON: According to 2 Samuel 14:27, Absalom had three sons (unnamed in the text) and one daughter named Tamar. All of Absalom's sons had died before him.

21. JOAB SAID TO THE CUSHITE: Cush was the area south of Egypt.

27. HE IS A GOOD MAN, AND COMES WITH GOOD NEWS: David believed the choice of the messenger indicated the content of the message.

29. I DID NOT KNOW: Ahimaaz, son of Zadok the priest, concealed his knowledge of Absalom's death just as Joab had requested.

32. LIKE THAT YOUNG MAN: The Cushite's reply was not so much indirect as culturally phrased (see a similar reference given in 1 Samuel 25:26).

33. O MY SON ABSALOM: David repeated the phrase "my son" five times in this verse as he lamented the death of Absalom. In spite of all the harm Absalom had caused to him and the nation of Israel, David was preoccupied with his personal loss in a melancholy way, which seems to be consistent with his weakness as a father.

*THE RETURN OF THE KING: As David prepares to return to his beloved city of Jerusalem, he also prepares to oust his commander— for a new one.*

19:1. THE KING IS WEEPING AND MOURNING FOR ABSALOM: Joab knew that David's throne would not be secure as long as Absalom was alive, and he acted in what he thought was the best interests for Israel by putting the young man to death. In doing this, he would have known that he would have to face David's wrath for going against his direct command.

3. AS PEOPLE WHO ARE ASHAMED: David's grief over the death of Absalom had a profound effect on his soldiers. They had risked their lives in battle, and many had also been forced to kill their fellow countrymen and perhaps even their own kinsmen in the civil war. They expected their leader to rejoice over the victory, but instead they were filled with shame and dismay.

5. TODAY YOU HAVE DISGRACED ALL YOUR SERVANTS: Once again, we see Joab confronting the king boldly and even aggressively. Joab may or may not have had David's best interests at heart, but he was concerned for Israel from a political standpoint.

6. YOU LOVE YOUR ENEMIES AND HATE YOUR FRIENDS: Joab could not grasp David's commitment to mercy and unity. David did not desire revenge

and bloodshed but longed for peace and a unified nation—though his application of those priorities was not always wise, as his failures to execute justice within his own household prove. Joab did not share David's convictions, and his immediate response was always to exact revenge. In this instance he was probably sickened to see his king weeping over a fallen enemy.

IT WOULD HAVE PLEASED YOU WELL: Of course, this was a ridiculous overstatement on Joab's part that it would have pleased David if all his troops had died. David was in a position where he could not avoid catastrophe: either he lost his throne (and his life), or he lost his son.

7. GO OUT AND SPEAK COMFORT TO YOUR SERVANTS: This was sound advice. David needed to honor his loyal soldiers for the cost they had paid in putting down the rebellion. Joab saw clearly that the king risked losing the people's support.

IF YOU DO NOT GO OUT, NOT ONE WILL STAY WITH YOU: Joab was a dangerous person because of his power. Here he was making a veiled threat that he would personally see to it that the army defected unless David stopped mourning. David knew he would be in deep trouble if he did not immediately express appreciation to his men for their victory.

8. SAT IN THE GATE: It was at the gate of Mahanaim that David had reviewed his troops as they had marched out to battle (see 2 Samuel 18:4). David's sitting in the gate represented a return to his exercise of kingly authority.

*AMASA'S APPOINTMENT: When the men of Judah, David's own tribe, refuse to accept him as their king, David seizes an opportunity to secure their loyalty and remove Joab from power.*

9. A DISPUTE THROUGHOUT ALL THE TRIBES: An argument arose in Israel as to whether David should be returned to the kingship. David's past military victories over the Philistines and the failure of Absalom argued for his return, so David's supporters insisted on knowing why their fellow Israelites remained quiet about returning David to his rightful place on the throne in Jerusalem.

11. ELDERS OF JUDAH: David appealed to the leaders of his own tribe of Judah to take the initiative in restoring him to the throne in Jerusalem. Although this appeal produced the desired result, it would also lead to some tribal jealousies (see 2 Samuel 19:40–43).

13. AMASA . . . MY BONE AND MY FLESH: Absalom had appointed Amasa as commander of the army of Israel, replacing Joab, who had accompanied David on his flight from Jerusalem. Amasa was the son of Abigail, either David's sister or his half sister (see 1 Chronicles 2:17), which made him David's nephew. His mother was also the sister of Zeruiah, the mother of Joab. Therefore, Amasa was a cousin of Absalom, Joab, and Abishai.

IN PLACE OF JOAB: David now appointed Amasa commander of his army in order to secure the allegiance of those who had followed him when he led Absalom's forces. The appointment did persuade the tribe of Judah to support David's return to the kingship, and it also secured the animosity of Joab against Amasa for taking his position.

15. CAME TO GILGAL: This town was located east of Jericho, but west of the Jordan. Gilgal was the place where Samuel had declared Saul to be king and where Saul had offered a sacrifice to the Lord without the prophet.

## UNLEASHING THE TEXT

1) Why did David command his three generals to deal gently with Absalom? What does this say about his weakness as a father?

_____

_____

_____

_____

2) Why did Joab kill Absalom? In your opinion, was this justified or unjustified? What were Joab's probable motives?

_____

_____

_____

_____

3) Why did Joab accuse David of loving his enemies and hating his friends? What does this reveal about the character of Joab?

_____

_____

_____

4) Why did David appoint Amasa in place of Joab? What issues did this solve for him? What issues did it create?

_____

_____

_____

## EXPLORING THE MEANING

***Vengeance belongs to God.*** The latter part of David's life was plagued by vengeful people. Absalom murdered his brother to get revenge for his sister's rape. Joab murdered Abner out of a spirit of vengefulness—and would soon go on to murder another man who had also not done him any personal wrong. Both murderers undoubtedly justified their crimes in their own minds, convinced they were accomplishing some "greater good" through their acts of violence. After all, both were avenging some perceived crime against their families, and both stood to gain personally from the deaths of their victims.

It is easy to justify sin in our own minds, but when we do, we fail to see our lives from God's perspective. Absalom may have felt aggrieved that Amnon was not punished for raping Tamar, but it was not his place to even the score. If he had seen the situation through God's eyes, he would have realized the Lord would address Amnon's guilt in His own time. Absalom was not responsible or qualified to bring justice; only God can do that.

When we take vengeance into our own hands, we only succeed in creating another injustice. Absalom did not amend the situation by addressing Amnon's sin. He only committed another sin and went on to bring the entire nation into civil war. Christians are called to repay evil with righteousness, not to exact justice on those who offend us (see Romans 12:19–21).

***Man's wrath does not produce God's righteousness.*** Absalom and Joab thought they could produce justice and righteousness through their violent acts. Absalom thought he was repaying a sin against his sister and leading the people in a better direction than his father had. Joab thought he was acting in Israel's interests and keeping David secure in his kingship. But their wrathful actions did not produce righteousness, only more sins and more anger.

Anger in itself is not wrong. It is an emotional response to circumstances, and there is a place for righteous wrath. Anger can be an indication that something is wrong in a relationship, and it can alert us to the fact that we need to address an issue with a brother or sister. The danger lies in what we do with our anger—and all too often it leads us into sin.

We are right to be angry at sin and mad at the wickedness in the world around us. But we are wrong when we take out our anger on other people, whether by word or deed. As such, we are warned, "Let every man be . . . slow to wrath; for the wrath of man does not produce the righteousness of God" (James 1:19–20) and further, "'Be angry, [but] do not sin': do not let the sun go down on your wrath" (Ephesians 4:26–27).

***Our sin can produce long-term suffering, but God's grace is greater.*** The Lord had declared that David's household would be fraught with treachery and violence, and that terrible prophecy came to pass through the sins of Amnon, Absalom, Joab, and others. David's throne and his very life were threatened by civil strife, power lusts, and revenge—and all these things were a result of his own sins of adultery and murder. One man's sins had a devastating effect on his entire household and on the entire nation of Israel.

Yet this is only part of the truth. The other part is equally important: God's grace overcomes the sins of men. David was a sinful man, and his deeds bore bitter fruit for many—yet God still used him to bring about the birth of Jesus Christ. The Lord had declared that David's throne would be established forever, and nothing could prevent God's promise from coming to pass. Even more, as horrific as David's sins were, the Bible still speaks of him as "a man after [God's] own heart" (Acts 13:22).

This does not give us license to sin, for the consequences of sin are real, as David's life demonstrates. Yet we can rejoice in the fact that the blood of Christ has covered *all* our sins and we are redeemed from eternal judgment and separation from God. "For as by one man's disobedience many were made sinners, so also by one Man's obedience many will be made righteous. Moreover the law entered that the offense might abound. But where sin abounded, grace abounded much more, so that as sin reigned in death, even so grace might reign through righteousness to eternal life through Jesus Christ our Lord" (Romans 5:19–21).

## REFLECTING ON THE TEXT

5) What events led to the failure of Absalom's rebellion? How was the hand of God at work in orchestrating all of the events?

_____

_____

_____

6) Why did Joab rebuke David for not commending his troops? How did David respond?

_____

_____

_____

7) Why was the tribe of Judah reluctant to take back David as their king? How did David seek to persuade them to his side?

_____

_____

_____

8) If you had been in Joab's place, how would you have reacted when David replaced you with Amasa? How would you have felt toward both of them?

_____

_____

_____

## PERSONAL RESPONSE

9) Are you harboring anger toward another person? What will you do this week to forgive that person? What will you do to improve your relationship?

_____

_____

_____

10) In what ways has God demonstrated His grace toward you? How can you imitate Him in your relationships with your family, your friends, and your coworkers?

_____

_____

_____

# 10

# A SECOND REBELLION
## *2 Samuel 19:16–20:26*

## DRAWING NEAR

What are some conflicts in your life that escalated because you didn't feel you were being treated fairly? How would you do things differently now?

_____

_____

_____

## THE CONTEXT

In a previous study, we saw how David had honored his promise to Jonathan by extending mercy to his son Mephibosheth. He not only spared Mephibosheth's life but extended him grace and invited him to sit at his own table. However, when David was forced to flee Jerusalem following Absalom's revolt, a rumor came through Ziba, Saul's former steward, that Mephibosheth was using the situation to stage a coup of his own (see 2 Samuel 16:1–3).

Ziba presented himself to David as a loyal servant, bearing gifts and promising that his household would follow David wherever he went. David did not have the ability to investigate the matter, so he made a rash judgment and awarded Ziba the entire estate belonging to Mephibosheth. One can hardly fault him, for Ziba's accusation sounded plausible and David had been betrayed by many loyal supporters. It was not until later, during the events in this study, that Mephibosheth had the chance to present his side of the story and vindicate himself.

When David was restored to the throne, both loyal friends and former enemies came to swear their allegiance to him. David desired to regain his rule without unnecessary bloodshed, so he offered forgiveness to his enemies and rewards to those who had been faithful to him. Yet all was not well in the land, and seeds of discontent still stirred beneath the surface. So it was that when a quarrel erupted between the tribes of Israel and Judah, it provided a spark for another uprising against David's rule.

In this study, we will trace the events leading up to this second uprising, see how it was put down, and learn a bit more about the character of the powerful general Joab.

## Keys to the Text

Read 2 Samuel 19:16–20:26, noting the key words and phrases indicated below.

> MEPHIBOSHETH'S REBUTTAL: *When David returns to Jerusalem, he is met by Mephibosheth, who is anxious to state his side of the story and vindicate himself in the king's eyes.*

16. SHIMEI THE SON OF GERA: A distant relative of Saul, from the tribe of Benjamin, who had cursed David as a "bloodthirsty man" and a "rogue" (see 2 Samuel 16:7). Shimei had declared that the loss of David's throne was God's retribution for the king's past sins, and David had accepted his curse as from the Lord. Here Shimei confessed his sin of cursing David and his life was spared.

20. HOUSE OF JOSEPH: This is a reference to Ephraim, the descendant of Joseph, a large tribe of Israel that was representative of the ten northern tribes.

24. MEPHIBOSHETH THE SON OF SAUL CAME DOWN TO MEET THE KING: Mephibosheth, the son of Jonathan and grandson of Saul, also met David. He came to David with great humility, generosity of spirit, and gratitude, recognizing all the good the king had done for him.

HE HAD NOT CARED FOR HIS FEET: Mephibosheth was disabled and may have required assistance in some of his personal care. But his disheveled appearance was about far more than having no servants to help him—he had deliberately neglected his outward appearance as a sign of his grief over David's suffering.

25. WHY DID YOU NOT GO WITH ME: Those who had remained loyal to David had fled Jerusalem with him. Anyone who remained in the city was immediately suspected of disloyalty. David's question was thus quite valid.

26. MY SERVANT DECEIVED ME: Mephibosheth began to expose the lies that his servant Ziba had told. He had intended to ride on a donkey to find David, but Ziba took advantage of his disability and rode out ahead of him to bear the false report.

28. ALL MY FATHER'S HOUSE WERE BUT DEAD MEN: All of Saul's family were dead except Mephibosheth, so this was accurate on a literal level. But Mephibosheth was referring to the fact that, under any other king, his own life would have been forfeit. As we saw previously, David had done something quite extraordinary in the world's eyes when he honored the grandson of the previous king instead of putting him to death.

WHAT RIGHT HAVE I: Mephibosheth's gratitude seems genuine. He recognized he had received great grace from the king and had no grounds for demanding anything further.

29. WHY DO YOU SPEAK ANYMORE OF YOUR MATTERS: In other words, "I give up! This is too complicated for me to sort out right now." David was overcome with grief over the death of Absalom, was faced with reestablishing his throne after the rebellion, and had countless people demanding his attention. He may also have seen that his previous decision to give the lands to Ziba was hasty, as he had not investigated the charges. With all that was going on, Mephibosheth's estate must have seemed rather insignificant to David at that moment.

YOU AND ZIBA DIVIDE THE LAND: David had previously given the estate of Saul to Mephibosheth to be farmed by Ziba, and then, when he was deceived, he gave it all to Ziba. Now he decided to divide Saul's estate between Ziba and Mephibosheth. He was evidently uncertain of the truth of Mephibosheth's story and too distracted to inquire fully into the matter. It probably seemed more sensible under the circumstances to allow Mephibosheth and Ziba to resolve the dispute themselves. However, if Mephibosheth was telling the truth, the decision was unjust. Ziba should have been punished for his false accusation, and Mephibosheth should have remained in possession of what was rightfully his.

30. LET HIM TAKE IT ALL: At this point, the truth of Mephibosheth's story became clear. He was not motivated by a desire for personal gain. In fact, he had little concern for his own possessions. His chief desire was to remain in the presence of the king, and he was content to forgive Ziba's treachery and let him keep his heart's desire. David's son Solomon would later execute a similar judgment in a dispute between two prostitutes who each claimed a baby was her own. Solomon offered to cut the baby in two, and the true mother was so horrified that she immediately volunteered to give the child to her rival (see 1 Kings 3:16–28).

*TRIBAL RIVALRY: As David continues toward Jerusalem, a dispute breaks out between the men of the tribes of Israel and the men of Judah.*

31. BARZILLAI THE GILEADITE: He was an aged, wealthy benefactor of David from Gilead, located on the east side of the Jordan River. David offered to let Barzillai live in Jerusalem as his guest, but Barzillai preferred to live out his last years in his own house.

37. YOUR SERVANT CHIMHAM: Probably a son of Barzillai. It is probable that David gave a portion of his estate in Bethlehem to this man and his descendants (see Jeremiah 41:17).

41. STOLEN YOU AWAY: Because only the troops of Judah had escorted David as he crossed over the Jordan River, the ten northern tribes complained to David that the men of Judah had "kidnapped" him from them.

42. A CLOSE RELATIVE OF OURS: The men of Judah answered the men of Israel by stating David was a member of their tribe. They denied they had taken advantage of their relationship to the king, as some from the northern tribes had done.

43. TEN SHARES IN THE KING: The men of Israel replied that they had a greater right to David, as there were ten northern tribes in contrast to the one tribe of Judah. This hostility between Israel and Judah led to rebellion and, eventually, to the division of the united kingdom.

*A SHORT CAREER: The conflict between the tribes leads to an uprising by a man named Sheba. When war breaks out, David gives his first orders to his new commander, Amasa.*

20:1. THERE HAPPENED TO BE THERE A REBEL: As we have seen, the people of Israel believed that the people of Judah had been presumptuous in leading David back to Jerusalem in victory—they felt they too should have been included in the victory celebration. It seems a petty quarrel, but there are always people who use minor slights for personal gain.

SHEBA THE SON OF BICHRI: This man was one such person. Although nothing is known of him, he must have been a person of considerable power and influence to so quickly form such an extensive rebellion. He belonged to Saul's tribe, where the adherents of Saul's dynasty were still plentiful, and he could see the disgust of the ten tribes for Judah's presumption in the restoration. As a result, he sought to overturn David's authority in Israel.

WE HAVE NO SHARE IN DAVID: Sheba's declaration that the northern tribes had no part in David's realm was similar to words later used in 1 Kings 12:16 when Israel seceded from the united kingdom under Jeroboam.

2. EVERY MAN OF ISRAEL DESERTED DAVID: Yet again we see the tragic fickleness of the human heart. Once the ten tribes withdrew, Judah was left alone to escort the king to Jerusalem. Disloyalty of the north would continue as long as Sheba lived.

3. HIS CONCUBINES: When David returned to Jerusalem, he confined his concubines to a life of abstinence because of their sexual relations with Absalom (see 2 Samuel 16:21–22).

4. WITHIN THREE DAYS: David told Amasa to assemble an army in three days to end the insurrection started by Sheba, but his general took longer. David needed the army to be reassembled quickly, because he knew the rebellion by Sheba could become an even worse threat than the one raised by Absalom.

6. TAKE YOUR LORD'S SERVANTS AND PURSUE HIM: When Amasa failed to follow the king's orders, David did not reinstate Joab but appointed Joab's brother Abishai as commander of his forces. Abishai was to take the army of Joab to pursue the rebel leader. Joab went also, determined to take vengeance on his rival Amasa.

7. ALL THE MIGHTY MEN. These men are listed in 2 Samuel 23:8–39. The term *mighty* emphasizes excellence or unusual quality. In the Old Testament, it is used to describe the excellence of a lion (see Proverbs 30:30), of good or bad men (see Genesis 10:9; 1 Chronicles 19:8), of giants (see Genesis 6:4), of angels (see Psalm 103:20), and even God (see Deuteronomy 10:17). The Scriptures state the mighty man is not victorious because of his strength but because of his understanding and knowledge of the Lord (see Jeremiah 9:23–24).

*Joab's Revenge: Joab accompanies the army David sends out to suppress the rebellion. Along the way he seizes the opportunity to get rid of the man who replaced him as general.*

8. Amasa came before them: By this time Amasa had amassed some forces. He marched rapidly and came first to Gibeon to assume the role of commander. It is possible that Joab purposely let the sword fall from its sheath as he approached Amasa. In this way, he could stoop as if to pick it up and salute the new general with his sword in hand, without generating any suspicion of his intent. Joab used this ploy to gain the position he needed to stab the new commander, whom he considered as usurping his post.

9. Are you in health, my brother: Joab and Amasa actually were cousins, and this greeting was an open declaration of peaceful intentions. Yet Joab betrayed Amasa with a kiss, just as Judas would later do with Jesus. Joab, who was present with his men, seized Amasa by his beard with his right hand, apparently to give the kiss of greeting. Instead, with his left hand, he thrust his sword into Amasa's stomach.

11. one of Joab's men: David's troops reinstated Joab as commander of the army. It is a striking demonstration of Joab's influence over the soldiers that he could murder the commander whom David had chosen—right before their eyes—and they would still unanimously follow him as their leader in pursuit of Sheba.

14. Abel and Beth Maachah: That is, the city of Abel Beth-Maacha, located about twenty-five miles north of the Sea of Galilee and four miles west of the city of Dan.

*Crisis Resolved: David's army chases the rebel Sheba to Abel Beth-Maacha and begins to lay seige to the city. But a wise woman offers Joab a solution to end the conflict and save her people.*

16. a wise woman cried out: This woman was probably a prominent judge in the city. She was making her appeal based on the laws of warfare recorded in Deuteronomy 20:10, which required the assaulting army to offer peace before making war. She pleaded for Joab to ask the city if they wanted peace and, thus, avert the coming bloodshed.

19. A MOTHER IN ISRAEL: This is a reference to a specially honored city or a recognized capital of the region.

THE INHERITANCE OF THE LORD: This refers to the land of Israel.

20. FAR BE IT FROM ME, THAT I SHOULD SWALLOW UP OR DESTROY: The ruthless general Joab was a patriot at heart who, after taking the leader of the insurrection, was ready to end further bloodshed. The woman eagerly responded with the promise of Sheba's head.

21. THE MOUNTAINS OF EPHRAIM: A large, partially forested plateau that extended into the tribal territory of Benjamin from the north.

23. JOAB WAS OVER ALL THE ARMY: David could not get rid of Joab, even though he hated him. He had to ignore the murder of Amasa and recognize Joab as army commander.

24. ADORAM WAS IN CHARGE OF REVENUE: He was in charge of the "revenue," a term used to describe the hard labor imposed on subjugated peoples. Adoram oversaw the forced labor on such projects as the building of highways, temples, and houses.

25. SHEVA WAS SCRIBE: He replaced Seraiah as David's secretary.

26. IRA THE JAIRITE WAS A CHIEF MINISTER: He was David's royal adviser.

## UNLEASHING THE TEXT

1) If you had been in David's position, how would you have responded to Ziba's accusations against Mephibosheth? How would you have responded to Mephibosheth's claims?

_____

_____

_____

_____

2) What was the source of the dispute between the tribes of Israel and Judah? How did this so suddenly lead to another rebellion?

_____

_____

_____

_____

3) What are the dangers of people following their own self-interests instead of God's will? How do you see this at work in the Israelites' lives?

_____

_____

_____

_____

4) Why did Joab murder Amasa? Why did the soldiers follow him after this brutal killing? What does this reveal about his personality and motivations?

_____

_____

_____

_____

## Exploring the Meaning

***Don't judge without all of the information.*** David was in a desperate state when he was forced to flee Jerusalem for his life. As king he was directly responsible for the welfare of those who remained loyal to him, and he also had to formulate plans on how to counteract Absalom's rebellion. He was being assailed by many people with many concerns, and he had to make quick decisions to send some ahead, some back, and some into enemy territory.

Given this, it is easy to understand why he made a hasty decision to accept Ziba's story at face value. After all, Ziba had brought him a generous gift of food and provisions for his men, and it might have made sense at the time that Mephibosheth would betray him. But that decision proved to be unjust, for Ziba's motives were not pure. It would have been far wiser for David to postpone judgment until he had the time to look into the facts behind the accusation. The results of this hasty decision could have been even worse, as Mephibosheth could have faced the death penalty for such treachery if Ziba's claims had proven true.

In Proverbs 18:17 we read, "The first one to plead his case seems right, until his neighbor comes and examines him." When people present their case, they always do so in the most favorable way so as to convince their listeners. But often the truth comes to light when the other side of the case is heard. For this reason, it is always wiser to postpone decision-making until we've had time to consult both sides of an issue, and to seek the Lord in prayer. Not only does God's grace overcome our human frailties, but He also promises to give wisdom whenever we ask. As James reminds us, "If any of you lacks wisdom, let him ask of God, who gives to all liberally and without reproach, and it will be given to him" (James 1:5).

**We are commanded to show mercy to those who wrong us.** Ziba was not the only one who sought to take advantage of David's apparent downfall. As David was fleeing Jerusalem, Shimei took the opportunity to curse David and even throw stones at him. At that time David refused to allow his men to kill Shimei, saying, "It may be that the LORD will look on my affliction, and that the LORD will repay me with good for his cursing this day" (2 Samuel 16:12).

Later, when the tables had turned and David was restored to power, Shimei hurried to travel with the men from Judah who were meeting David on his way back to Jerusalem. Shimei fell down before the king, admitted that he had sinned, and begged for mercy. Once again David's men desired to kill Shimei, but the king replied, "Shall any man be put to death today in Israel? For do I not know that today I am king over Israel?" (19:22).

In sparing Shimei's life at this time, and not seeking retribution for Ziba's false accusation, David was demonstrating the kind of mercy he had extended to King Saul and Mephibosheth when he had spared their lives. Likewise, Mephibosheth did not try to get even with Ziba, though the crime of which he had been accused carried the death penalty. At the very least, Mephibosheth could have demanded that all his lands and possessions be returned to him. But instead he showed mercy and gave Ziba the possessions he had coveted.

In extending mercy, both David and Mephibosheth were demonstrating principles taught by Jesus: "Judge not, and you shall not be judged. Condemn not, and you shall not be condemned. Forgive, and you will be forgiven. Give, and it will be given to you: good measure, pressed down, shaken together, and running over will be put into your bosom. For with the same measure that you use, it will be measured back to you" (Luke 6:37–38).

**We are called to put aside petty jealousies that lead to quarrels.** When we look at the source of the conflict that led to Sheba's rebellion, the cause seems to be a petty dispute between the tribes over who had the right to escort David back to Jerusalem. On the one side, the men of Judah claimed they had the right because David belonged to their tribe. On the other side, the men of Israel said they had the right because they had "ten shares in the king" (2 Samuel 19:43). They represented more tribes, so they should have been consulted in bringing him back.

Shortly after, Sheba called the tribes of Israel to revolt, saying, "We have *no share* in David, nor do we have inheritance in the son of Jesse" (20:1, emphasis added). Clearly, the animosity between the two groups had been brewing for some time, and the return of David provided the trigger that set off the conflict. Had the tribes instead sought to work out their differences before exchanging harsh words and taking action, they would have spared the people yet another series of bloody battles and civil war.

James would later address this issue when he wrote, "Where do wars and fights come from among you? Do they not come from your desires for pleasure that war in your members? . . . But He gives more grace. Therefore He says: 'God resists the proud, but gives grace to the humble'" (James 4:1, 6). It is human nature to want to retaliate when we feel we are being overlooked or treated unfairly, but God calls us to work out our differences with humility.

## REFLECTING ON THE TEXT

5) In what ways did David and Mephibosheth show mercy to those who had wronged them? In what ways do they illustrate Christlike character?

_____

_____

_____

_____

6) How could the tribes of Israel and Judah have resolved their dispute before it led to further bloodshed and strife in the land? What would have been a better course?

_____

_____

_____

_____

7) Why was David so anxious to raise up an army to suppress Sheba? Why did he so quickly replace Amasa when he failed to assemble the men of Judah in three days?

_____

_____

_____

_____

8) How do you view the actions of the wise woman of Abel Beth-Maacha? Why do you think the city was willing to go along with the execution of Sheba?

_____

_____

_____

## Personal Response

9) What decisions in your life require wisdom at present? What steps will you take to ensure that you make a wise decision?

_____

_____

_____

10) What are some conflicts that are brewing in your life at the moment? How can you show humility in those situations and seek to work out your differences?

_____

_____

_____

# 11

# THE MAN AFTER GOD'S HEART

*2 Samuel 22:1–23:7*

## DRAWING NEAR

What does it mean to you to be a person "after God's heart"? What characteristics does such an individual possess?

_____

_____

_____

## THE CONTEXT

In these studies, we have seen David commit some grievous sins, and we have witnessed the terrible results of those offenses. He committed adultery with Bathsheba, murdered Uriah, and then tried to cover up those sins and continue on with his life as though he'd done nothing wrong. He failed to punish Amnon when he raped Tamar, and he failed to take action against Absalom when he sought revenge and murdered Amnon.

In spite of this, Paul would later say, "[God] raised up for them David as king, to whom also He gave testimony and said, 'I have found David the son of Jesse, a man after My own heart, who will do all My will'" (Acts 13:22). At first glance, this seems like a contradiction. How can a murderer and adulterer be a man after God's own heart? To understand this, we must actually look at David's whole life, not merely a certain season of sin. We must also remember that *all* people sin—including Christians, who have the Holy Spirit living within them.

In this study, we will look at the events of David's final years on earth and address this question of what it means to be a person after God's own heart. We will look at two songs of praise that David composed to express his thanksgiving for God's deliverance and great salvation. We will discover that David's heart was always turned toward the Lord, and that he was eager to restore his relationship with God after he sinned. In this, we will learn that anyone can be a person after God's own heart by keeping God first in every area of life.

## KEYS TO THE TEXT

Read 2 Samuel 22:1–23:7, noting the key words and phrases indicated below.

> GOD MY DELIVERER: *David composes a song to praise the Lord for His continual protection and deliverance. He states that he places his security in the fortress of God's love.*

22:1. THE LORD HAD DELIVERED HIM FROM THE HAND OF ALL HIS ENEMIES: David likely wrote this psalm toward the end of his life, after the Lord had given him victory over the Philistines and other enemies of Israel, though some scholars date it earlier in his reign.

2. THE LORD IS MY ROCK: This introduction contains the sum and substance of the whole psalm. David extols God as his defense, his refuge, and his deliverer in the many experiences of his agitated life. The rock is used as a metaphor for the Lord throughout Scripture. It depicts something solid, immovable, and unchanging—a stable anchor amid life's storms. Jesus is also pictured as the cornerstone on which the kingdom of God is built as well as a stone of stumbling (see 1 Peter 2:6–8).

MY FORTRESS AND MY DELIVERER: The author previously used this term to describe the citadel of Jerusalem (see 2 Samuel 5:9) and the cave of Adullam (see 1 Samuel 22:1). Like those strongholds, God had been a consistent defender and a safe place of refuge throughout David's tumultuous life, and David praised God for repeatedly delivering him from his enemies.

HORN OF MY SALVATION: A symbol of strength and power.

MY STRONGHOLD AND MY REFUGE: A secure, lofty retreat that the enemy finds inaccessible. As such, the Lord is the refuge of His chosen one, secure from all hostile attacks.

4. I WILL CALL UPON THE LORD: This was a characteristic of David's life—to call on the Lord in all circumstances. David called on God after he sinned, as we saw in a previous study, and he called on Him in praise and adoration, as we see here.

5. WAVES OF DEATH: David pictures these waves as violent floods of water ready to break over him and as traps set by a hunter to snare him. As we have seen, David faced the reality of imminent death throughout his personal experience, most frequently when pursued by Saul, but also in Absalom's conspiracy and in certain wars.

7. IN MY DISTRESS I CALLED UPON THE LORD: The particular trouble David was referring to here was the potential of his imminent death. David also called on the Lord when he needed help and strength. In all his calling, he was always confident that the Lord heard him—and he was never disappointed.

8. HE WAS ANGRY: This picture of God's wrath is both terrifying and accurate (see Revelation 19:11–21), but David also recognized he would not face that fury. Christians can likewise rest in the assurance that they will never face the wrathful judgment of God.

14. THE LORD THUNDERED: In a literal manner, the Lord did to His enemies what Hannah, the mother of Samuel, said He would do in her prayer: "The adversaries of the LORD shall be broken in pieces; from heaven He will thunder against them. The LORD will judge the ends of the earth. He will give strength to His king, and exalt the horn of His anointed" (1 Samuel 2:10).

*THE CHARACTER OF GOD: David praises God for who He is, rejoicing in His perfect character.*

17. HE SENT FROM ABOVE: Jesus literally fulfilled this picture when He descended from heaven and took on human form to redeem His people from death—the strongest of man's enemies.

20. HE DELIVERED ME BECAUSE HE DELIGHTED IN ME: David was not suggesting he was worthy of God's favor, but that God delivered him simply because He chose to do so—and He delighted in him because He is a God of love.

21. **The Lord rewarded me according to my righteousness:** David was not claiming in this passage that he was inherently righteous or free from sin. Indeed, if he wrote this psalm later in his life, he was well aware of his sinful nature. The righteousness of which he was speaking was his basic desire to obey God's Word. He had a heart to please God, and the Lord was faithful to bless him throughout his life.

22. **I have kept the ways of the Lord:** Here is another element of being a man after God's own heart: obedience. David certainly committed sin, but his life overall was characterized by faithfulness to God's directions.

23. **All His judgments were before me:** The man after God's own heart will spend time on a regular basis studying God's Word.

24. **I was also blameless before Him:** Again, this does not mean that David was free from sin; it just means that God had forgiven his sins, removed them from the record, and blotted them out. When we confess our sins, God always forgives us—He blots out our sins and eliminates them from His mind. Christians still miss the mark, but our sins are completely covered by the blood of Christ, and God sees us through that blood as righteous before Him.

26. **With the merciful You will show Yourself merciful:** We do not earn God's favor through our own righteousness. Rather, God is always working to lead us into righteousness. The Lord encourages mercy and humility, because those are His own characteristics, and He resists ungodly behavior in an attempt to move sinners toward Himself.

28. **Your eyes are on the haughty:** God seeks to "bring them down" not because He is looking for an excuse to judge, but because He wants the proud to humble themselves before Him. "When they cast you down, and you say, 'Exaltation will come!' Then He will save the humble person. He will even deliver one who is not innocent; yes, he will be delivered by the purity of your hands" (Job 22:29–30).

29. **My lamp:** David as the "lamp" of Israel reflected the light of the glory of God, who was the "Lamp" of David himself.

36. **The shield of Your salvation:** This description summarizes all that God is to His people. He saves those who belong to Him from eternal judgment and protects them from the enemy of their souls.

50. **Among the Gentiles:** Paul would later quote this passage in Romans 15:8–9 when he wrote, "Jesus Christ has become a servant to the circumcision for the truth of God, to confirm the promises made to the fathers, and

that the Gentiles might glorify God for His mercy, as it is written: 'For this reason I will confess to You among the Gentiles, and sing to Your name.'"

51. HIS KING . . . HIS ANOINTED: These terms are singular and thus do not seem to refer to David and his descendants. Rather, they refer to the promised "seed," the coming Messiah. At the end of David's life, he looked back in faith at God's promises and forward in hope to their fulfillment in the coming of a future king, the "anointed one."

DAVID'S LEGACY: *At the end of his life, David reflects on how the Lord has used him for His glory and how the Lord has established with him an everlasting covenant.*

23:1. THE LAST WORDS OF DAVID: This is David's final literary legacy to Israel, not his final oral speech (which is recorded in 1 Kings 2:1–10).

THUS SAYS: Literally "declares as an oracle," in much the same way that Balaam declared an oracle concerning God's word for His people (see Numbers 24:3, 15). David realized the psalms he wrote, as directed by the Holy Spirit, were the very Word of God.

2. THE SPIRIT OF THE LORD: God's Holy Spirit is the divine instrument of revelation and inspiration (see 2 Timothy 3:16; 2 Peter 1:19–21).

3. HE WHO RULES OVER MEN: These words begin the record of direct speech from God, whose ideal king must exercise His authority with justice and in complete submission to His divine sovereignty. Such a king is like the helpful rays of the sun at dawn and the life-giving showers that nourish the earth. The Old Testament writers and prophets identified this ideal king as the coming Messiah. "For unto us a Child is born, unto us a Son is given; and the government will be upon His shoulder. And His name will be called Wonderful, Counselor, Mighty God, Everlasting Father, Prince of Peace" (Isaiah 9:6–7).

5. MY HOUSE IS NOT SO WITH GOD: In response to God's standard for His ideal king, David confessed that his house had not always ruled over the people of Israel in righteousness and in the fear of God. Thus, his house was not the fulfillment of God's words in 2 Samuel 7:12–16. Furthermore, none of the kings of David's line (according to 1–2 Kings) would meet God's standard of righteous obedience.

HE HAS MADE WITH ME AN EVERLASTING COVENANT: The promise God gave to David in 2 Samuel 7:12–16 is here referred to as a "covenant"—a binding agreement from the Lord that He will fulfill. In spite of the fact that David and his own household had failed, David rightly believed the Lord would not fail but would be faithful to His promise of future hope through David's seed. This eternal King would establish a kingdom of righteousness and peace forever.

6. SONS OF REBELLION: Literally, "sons of Belial." The wicked enemies of God will be cast aside in judgment when the Messiah, the fulfillment of the Davidic covenant, establishes His rule on the earth (see Isaiah 63:1–6).

## GOING DEEPER

Read Psalm 72 and note the key words and phrase indicated below.

*A PRAYER: It is believed David wrote this psalm as a prayer for Solomon, through his words keep the future reign of the Messiah in sight.*

72.1. A PSALM OF SOLOMON: It is not known whether David or Solomon was the author of this psalm. The last verse seems to indicate it is the last prayer psalm David wrote, and the inscription "of Solomon" could be interpreted "about Solomon." Regardless, the psalm is dedicated to the prosperity of Solomon at the beginning of his reign (see 1 Kings 2).

GIVE THE KING YOUR JUDGMENTS: A prayer that the king would faithfully mediate God's justice on the nation.

THE KING'S SON: This primarily refers to Solomon, emphasizing his bond with the Davidic dynasty, but it also anticipates the Messiah's reign as the culmination of the Davidic covenant. Although no New Testament writer applies any of the words of this psalm to Christ, the messianic inferences should not be missed. This psalm describes a reign when God, the king, nature, all classes of society, and foreign nations will live together in harmony.

3. MOUNTAINS WILL BRING PEACE: When the king rules with justice and compassion, the earth radiates well-being.

7. UNTIL THE MOON IS NO MORE: This refers to the length of the Davidic dynasty and, possibly, to the messianic reign (see 2 Samuel 7:16; Luke 1:32–33).

8. THE RIVER: Israel's boundaries were to extend to the River Euphrates (see Exodus 23:31; 1 Kings 4:21; Psalm 89:25).

10. KINGS OF TARSHISH . . . KINGS OF SHEBA AND SEBA: These are countries, near and far, that brought tribute to Solomon. Tarshish was probably

in Spain, Sheba was a kingdom in southern Arabia (modern-day Yemen), and Seba was a North African nation.

20. THE PRAYERS OF DAVID . . . ARE ENDED: Asaph's psalms immediately follow after this (Psalms 73–83), though David did author some of the psalms included later in the collection.

## UNLEASHING THE TEXT

1) On what basis did David hope to find mercy from God? Why was he so confident that God would extend mercy to him even though he was a sinner?

_____

_____

_____

_____

2) What are some of the ways that David depicted God in his song in 2 Samuel 22?

_____

_____

_____

3) According to this passage from 2 Samuel 22, why did God deliver David from his enemies? Why did God show His wrath to those people?

_____

_____

_____

4) What words did God give to David in 2 Samuel 23:3–4? How did David acknowledge the failure of his own house to live up to God's standards of righteous obedience?

_____

_____

_____

_____

## EXPLORING THE MEANING

**_When we confess our sins, God utterly blots them out._** David's sins against God were dreadful. These offenses brought judgment on his entire household and resulted in sowing discord and rebellion within his kingdom. God's law demanded the death penalty for both adultery and murder, and David was condemned twice over. Yet God did not put him to death but instead "put away" David's sin and blotted it out of existence. David still faced temporal consequences of those sins, but he was set free from the judgment and wrath of God.

However, God did not show David such grace and mercy until he repented of his sins. David thought he could hide his sin, and for many months he went about his life as though he had done nothing wrong. During that time he was not at peace. "When I kept silent," he wrote, "my bones grew old through my groaning all the day long. For day and night Your hand was heavy upon me; my vitality was turned into the drought of summer" (Psalm 32:3–4). Yet the moment he confessed his sin and repented, he found peace and restoration with God.

The Lord, speaking through the prophet Jeremiah, said of His people, "I will forgive their iniquity, and their sin I will remember no more" (Jeremiah 31:34). God desires unbroken fellowship with all people, and He is quick to forget our trespasses. The important element in this is that God's people should also be quick to confess their sins. "If we confess our sins, He is faithful and just to forgive us our sins and to cleanse us from all unrighteousness" (1 John 1:9).

***Christians may face discipline, but we will never face God's angry judgment.***
The wrathful judgment of God refers to His ultimate sentence of eternal separation from Himself. This sentence falls on any who die in their sin, because God cannot tolerate sin in His presence. The Bible teaches that all people have sinned and that no one can eradicate the sin nature. We are all descended from Adam, and therefore we all share Adam's sinful nature—there is nothing we can do to remove that likeness.

However, the good news is that what we cannot do, God can! He sent His Son to become a man, born of the Spirit of God. Jesus was not subject to death because He had never sinned, yet He willingly died on the cross to pay the penalty for *our* sins. When we accept Christ's atonement for our sins, we are born again into the family of God—and nothing can ever remove us from that family. The Lord does discipline us in order to produce godly character in our lives, but this is not the same as facing eternal judgment.

Once we have been born again into Jesus Christ, nothing can ever separate us from Him. Paul wrote, "For God did not appoint us to wrath, but to obtain salvation through our Lord Jesus Christ, who died for us, that whether we wake or sleep, we should live together with Him" (1 Thessalonians 5:9–10). He also declared, "I am persuaded that neither death nor life, nor angels nor principalities nor powers, nor things present nor things to come, nor height nor depth, nor any other created thing, shall be able to separate us from the love of God which is in Christ Jesus our Lord" (Romans 8:38–39).

***God is always working to draw people to Himself.*** God's wrath is a terrible thing to contemplate, as we see in the vivid word pictures that David drew in his songs. The Lord is angered by injustice and unrighteousness. He resists the proud and turns deviousness back on itself. His voice thunders and His breath blazes forth, consuming all the wicked deeds of men.

Yet God takes no delight in pouring out His wrath, and His goal is always to bring the sinner to repentance. His "eyes are on the haughty," David wrote, that He "may bring them down" (2 Samuel 22:28)—that is, that the proud might become humble. God does not look for excuses to destroy people. Rather, He looks to draw His children to Himself and make them more like Christ. This does not discount the fact that God's wrath will fall on those who die apart from Christ, but while a person is alive, God's grace and salvation are always available—and the Lord uses every means to draw the sinner to Himself.

Once saved, the Christian is *permanently* saved from God's wrath. Thus, for Christians, God's anger toward sin is always expressed as discipline intended to make us more like His Son. If we will submit to God's discipline, we will be conformed to Christ's image: "Now no chastening seems to be joyful for the present, but painful; nevertheless, afterward it yields the peaceable fruit of righteousness to those who have been trained by it" (Hebrews 12:11).

## REFLECTING ON THE TEXT

5) What word pictures did David use to describe God's wrath? To describe God's grace and mercy?

_____

_____

_____

6) What does it mean to "blot out" one's transgressions? Why does God do this? What is required of us?

_____

_____

_____

7) How does David describe the "king's Son" in Psalm 72? What similarities do you find between this psalm and David's depiction of the ideal king in 2 Samuel 23:3–4?

_____

_____

_____

8) How does David's prayer in Psalm 72 portray the reign of his son Solomon? How do his words further describe the glorious reign of the coming Messiah?

_____

_____

_____

## PERSONAL RESPONSE

9) Are you a person after God's own heart? What is involved in being such a person? How can you strengthen that quality this week?

_____

_____

_____

10) As you look back on your life, in what ways can you thank God for His guidance and deliverance? Take some time to praise God for His mercy in your life.

_____

_____

_____

# 12

# REVIEWING KEY PRINCIPLES

## DRAWING NEAR

As you look back at each of the studies in 2 Samuel, what is the one thing that stood out to you the most? What is one new perspective you have learned?

_____

_____

_____

## THE CONTEXT

From the past eleven studies, you have gained an overview of the reign of Israel's great King David. In the process you have met a variety of people whose lives were both good and bad. Together, we have admired David's skillful leadership and been shocked at his profound weaknesses. We have considered Joab, a valiant soldier who was also a treacherous murderer. We saw David mourn over the destruction of his household as he watched young men with great potential suffer tragic deaths. But one theme has remained constant throughout these studies: _God is faithful_, and those who obey Him will grow in faithfulness as they become capable of being men and women _after God's own heart_.

Someone who is "after God's own heart" sets the Lord's will above all other considerations. David demonstrated this characteristic, even though he sinned greatly. When he was confronted with his wickedness, he repented immediately and sought to be restored to an open relationship with God. Joab, in contrast, frequently put his own desires ahead of obedience to God, which is indicative of a person whose heart is not given fully to the Lord.

Here are a few of the major principles we have found during our study. There are many more we don't have room to reiterate, so take some time to review the earlier studies—or, better still, to meditate on the Scripture that we have covered. As you do, ask the Holy Spirit to give you wisdom and insight into His Word. He will not refuse.

## EXPLORING THE MEANING

**Division is the devil's tool.** The nation of Israel divided when King Saul died, with each faction placing their allegiance behind a different successor to the throne. That same division would return during David's reign and would ultimately divide Israel into two separate nations. Each time the people were divided, strife and civil war resulted.

Satan's goal is to divide God's people, because he knows that if we are busy contending against one another, we won't be doing battle against his forces of darkness. The evil one loves to see us bickering and scratching at one another, and he will do all he can to cause division and contention within the church. He knows that a united body of believers is a powerful force for advancing God's kingdom on earth.

The Lord wants His people to function as one body, to focus on serving one another, and to care for one another as members of that body. As Paul wrote, "Now I plead with you, brethren, by the name of our Lord Jesus Christ, that you all speak the same thing, and that there be no divisions among you, but that you be perfectly joined together in the same mind and in the same judgment . . . For where there are envy, strife, and divisions among you, are you not carnal and behaving like mere men? For when one says, 'I am of Paul,' and another, 'I am of Apollos,' are you not carnal?" (1 Corinthians 1:10; 3:3–4).

**The Lord is eager to bless, not to punish.** David was filled with fear of God's anger when he failed to follow the Lord's prescribed method of carrying the ark, and that fear hindered his ministry. But the Lord was not looking for excuses to display His wrath. Rather, He was eager to bless the people and lead them into righteousness and obedience. He poured out blessings upon the household of Obed-Edom just as He longed to do for the entire nation of Israel.

Our sin can cause us to have an inaccurate perspective of God's character. We can fall into the error of thinking that God is an angry being who looks for shortcomings and failures in the lives of His people and then eagerly punishes and rebukes them for it. The truth is just the opposite. The Lord *longs* to bless His people, and He is always looking for ways to demonstrate His love toward us.

The ultimate example of this is found in Christ. If God had been eager to punish us, He might have simply condemned the entire human race to eternal punishment, since that is precisely what our sins deserved. But instead God sent His own Son to die on the cross to pay the penalty for those sins and enabled us to be restored to fellowship with Him. As David himself wrote, "The LORD is merciful and gracious, slow to anger, and abounding in mercy. He will not always strive with us, nor will He keep His anger forever. He has not dealt with us according to our sins, nor punished us according to our iniquities" (Psalm 103:8–10).

***God's dealings with humankind are through His grace, not man's merit.*** Saul was king over Israel prior to David, but his entire reign was characterized by pride. He evidently felt that he had somehow merited being king and could order events as he saw fit. This attitude led him into many grievous sins, including attempts to murder David and consulting a witch for guidance instead of God.

David's life, in contrast, was characterized by humility (with a few significant lapses). As a rule, David recognized he had no merit in himself that deserved God's favor. God promised to establish his throne forever, and even brought the Messiah into the world through his descendants, but David understood He did these things simply because He chose to do so, not because David had somehow earned God's esteem.

God blesses His people because He loves them and it is in His very nature to do so. He forgives us because He chooses to forgive, and because His character is forgiving and gracious. No human being can ever earn God's blessings, and no person can ever make atonement for his or her sins. As Paul wrote, "For by grace you have been saved through faith, and that not of yourselves; it is the gift of God, not of works, lest anyone should boast" (Ephesians 2:8–9).

**We must fulfill our promises.** David and Jonathan loved one another like brothers, and either would willingly have laid down his life for the other. In fact, Jonathan did risk his life by protecting David against Saul's murderous plans. The two men swore an oath of friendship, and David promised Jonathan that he would always show kindness to him and his family.

But Jonathan died young, fighting bravely against overwhelming odds with the Philistines. David, on the other hand, became king and had battles of his own to deal with. From the world's perspective, he would have been well within his kingly rights to put Mephibosheth to death so he would not prove a menace to his throne. In the world's eyes, it would have been more than gracious for David to simply ignore Mephibosheth and let him live. But David took his oath and promise to Jonathan seriously. He went beyond what was merely expected and deliberately showed compassion to Jonathan's son.

In this David was imitating the character of God, who always keeps His promises. As God's people, we too should take care to fulfill our word, whether it is given as a solemn oath (as in marriage vows) or a simple promise. To not do so invites divine judgment. In fact, according to James, it is better to not give your word at all than to give it and not keep it. "But above all, my brethren, do not swear, either by heaven or by earth or with any other oath. But let your 'Yes' be 'Yes,' and your 'No,' 'No,' lest you fall into judgment" (James 5:12).

**Sin breeds more sin.** David's problems began when he indulged his flesh and avoided the responsibilities of leading his army in battle. This led to a temptation he would have most likely avoided otherwise. He sinned openly when he gazed on Bathsheba during her bath, which inflamed his lust. This lust led to the sin of sexual immorality with a woman who was not his wife, which led him to err further by trying to hide his guilt from the people around him. And this sin led to the sin of murder.

It is important to understand that David alone was responsible for this tragic sequence of sin. The book of James bears this out: "Let no one say when he is tempted, 'I am tempted by God'; for God cannot be tempted by evil, nor does He Himself tempt anyone. But each one is tempted when he is drawn away by *his own* desires and enticed. Then, when desire has conceived, it gives birth to sin; and sin, when it is full-grown, brings forth *death*" (1:13–15, emphasis added). David made one bad decision, which led to another bad decision, and another—and the end result was the death of many innocent men.

Like David, we can find ourselves in a downward spiral of sin when we indulge our fleshly desires. The good news, however, is that God offers grace to cover our sin and the Holy Spirit to convict us of sin—and to help us avoid it in the first place.

**God's people must view sin from God's perspective.** When David committed adultery, he viewed his actions from a human perspective. His major concern was to prevent other people from knowing what he had done, which led him to attempt a cover-up. As we have seen already, however, his cover-up led to more sin and further attempts to conceal it.

If David had viewed his sin of adultery from God's point of view, he would have been quick to confess and repent. Humans are concerned with what other people will think, but God is interested in how our sin damages our relationship with Him. David was worried about his reputation as king, while God was thinking of his eternal fellowship.

Today, the world tells us the most important priority is appearances. The world tells us to place value on outward show and claims there are no eternal consequences for our actions. God, however, is focused on eternity. He wants His people to see every sin as something that puts distance between them and Him.

**Beware of ungodly counsel.** Jonadab saw that Amnon was pining away after a woman, so he offered advice on how to gratify his carnal cravings. And, like most false counselors, he seemed to be well versed in the intrigues of everyone around him, appearing at the most opportune times to give his advice, as he did when David was grieving.

Jonadab began his counsel to Amnon by suggesting that the young man deceive his father. He said, "Lie down on your bed and pretend to be ill. And when your father comes to see you, say to him, 'Please let my sister Tamar come and give me food, and prepare the food in my sight, that I may see it and eat it from her hand'" (2 Samuel 13:5). Amnon should have recognized that Jonadab's advice was ungodly and rejected it outright. Instead, he followed Jonadab's poisonous "wisdom," though he was not compelled to do so.

Today, the world bombards us with ungodly counsel that, like Jonadab's advice, often sounds wise and expedient. But God's people are called to weigh every teaching against the teachings of Scripture, and godly counsel never advises us to disobey God's commands. Had Amnon considered that fact, he may actually have succeeded his father on the throne.

***Vengeance belongs to God.*** The latter part of David's life was plagued by vengeful people. Absalom murdered his brother to get revenge for his sister's rape. Joab murdered Abner out of a spirit of vengefulness and would soon go on to murder another man who had also not done him any personal wrong. Both murderers undoubtedly justified their crimes in their own minds, convinced they were accomplishing some "greater good" through their acts of violence. After all, both were avenging some perceived crime against their families—and both stood to gain personally from the deaths of their victims.

It is easy to justify sin in our own minds, but when we do, we fail to see our lives from God's perspective. Absalom may have felt aggrieved that Amnon was not punished for raping Tamar, but it was not his place to even the score. If he had seen the situation through God's eyes, he would have realized the Lord would address Amnon's guilt in His own time. Absalom was not responsible or qualified to bring justice; only God can do that.

When we take vengeance into our own hands, we only succeed in creating another injustice. Absalom did not amend the situation by addressing Amnon's sin. He only committed another sin and went on to bring the entire nation into civil war. Christians are called to repay evil with righteousness, not to exact justice on those who offend us (see Romans 12:19–21).

## UNLEASHING THE TEXT

1) Which of the concepts or principles in this study have you found to be the most encouraging? Why?

_____

_____

_____

2) Which of the concepts or principles have you found most challenging? Why?

_____

_____

_____

3) What aspects of "walking with God" are you already doing in your life? Which areas need strengthening?

_____

_____

_____

4) To which of the characters that we've studied have you most been able to relate? How might you emulate that person in your own life?

_____

_____

_____

## PERSONAL RESPONSE

5) Have you taken a definite stand for Jesus Christ? Have you accepted His free gift of salvation? If not, what is preventing you from doing so?

_____

_____

_____

6) In which areas of your life have you been most convicted during this study? What exact things will you do to address these convictions? Be specific.

_____

_____

_____

7) What have you learned about the character of God during this study? How has this insight affected your worship or prayer life?

_____

_____

_____

8) What are some specific things you want to see God do in your life in the coming month? What are some things you intend to change in your own life during that time? (Return to this list in one month and hold yourself accountable to fulfill these things.)

_____

_____

_____

If you would like to continue in your study of the Old Testament, read the next title in this series: *1 Kings 1–11, Proverbs & Ecclesiastes: The Rise and Fall of Solomon.*

# ALSO AVAILABLE

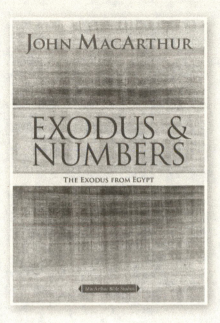

JOHN MACARTHUR

EXODUS & NUMBERS

THE EXODUS FROM EGYPT

MacArthur Bible Studies

In this study, John MacArthur guides readers through an in-depth look at the historical period beginning with God's calling of Moses, continuing through the giving of the Ten Commandments, and concluding with the Israelites' preparations to enter the Promised Land. This study includes close-up examinations of Aaron, Caleb, Joshua, Balaam and Balak, as well as careful considerations of doctrinal themes such as "Complaints and Rebellion" and "Following God's Law."

The MacArthur Bible Studies provide intriguing examinations of the whole of Scripture. Each guide incorporates extensive commentary, detailed observations on overriding themes, and probing questions to help you study the Word of God with guidance from John MacArthur.

# ALSO AVAILABLE

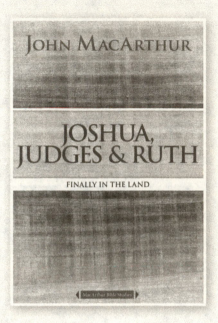

JOHN MACARTHUR

JOSHUA, JUDGES & RUTH

FINALLY IN THE LAND

‹ MacArthur Bible Studies ›

In this study, John MacArthur guides readers through an in-depth look at the Israelites' conquest of the Promised Land, beginning with the miraculous parting of the Jordan River, continuing through the victories and setbacks as the people settled into Canaan, and concluding with the time of the judges. Studies include close-up examinations of Rahab, Ruth, and Samson, as well as careful considerations of doctrinal themes such as "The Sin of Achan" and the role of "The Kinsman Redeemer."

The MacArthur Bible Studies provide intriguing examinations of the whole of Scripture. Each guide incorporates extensive commentary, detailed observations on overriding themes, and probing questions to help you study the Word of God with guidance from John MacArthur.

# ALSO AVAILABLE

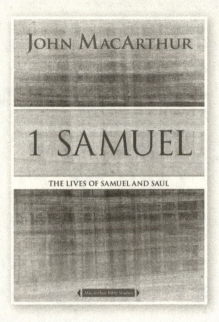

In this study, John MacArthur guides readers through an in-depth look at this historical period beginning with the miraculous birth of Samuel, continuing through Saul's crowning as Israel's first king, and concluding with his tragic death. Studies include close-up examinations of Hannah, Eli, Saul, David, and Jonathan, as well as careful considerations of doctrinal themes such as "Slaying a Giant" and "Respecting God's Anointed."

The MacArthur Bible Studies provide intriguing examinations of the whole of Scripture. Each guide incorporates extensive commentary, detailed observations on overriding themes, and probing questions to help you study the Word of God with guidance from John MacArthur.

# ALSO AVAILABLE

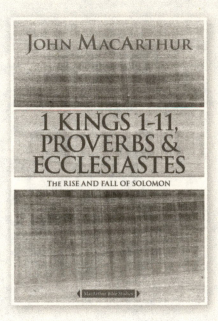

In this study, John MacArthur guides readers through an in-depth look at the historical period beginning with Solomon's ascent to the throne and continuing through his tragic end. Studies include close-up examinations of the vital importance of wisdom—with portraits of the wise woman, the foolish sluggard, and others in the book of Proverbs—and careful considerations of doctrinal themes such as "True Wisdom from God" and "A Time for Everything."

The MacArthur Bible Studies provide intriguing examinations of the whole of Scripture. Each guide incorporates extensive commentary, detailed observations on overriding themes, and probing questions to help you study the Word of God with guidance from John MacArthur.